25 NUGGETS AT
Twenty five

SECRETS TO GODLY MARRIAGE

25 Nuggets at *Twenty five*

2020

1995

Dedication

To the late Mr. Emmanuel George Ofori and Madam Esther Tenkorang and Mr. Isaac Kwamina De-Graft Takyi and Auntie Alberta Aduffua Agyapong. Our beloved parents who taught us by their example that marriage is for life.

CONTENTS

Chapter 1. Marriage Prayer 1

Chapter 2. 25 Marriage Definitions to Note 7

Chapter 3. 25 Marriage Scriptures to Reflect On 17

Chapter 4. 25 Marriage Quotes to Add To 30

Chapter 5. 25 Reasons Why Marriages Fail 37
    1. *Unforgiving Spirit* 38
    2. *Financial Pressure* 39
    3. *Infidelity* 40
    4. *Insecurity and Worry* 40
    5. *Secret Sins* 40
    6. *Parenting Differences* 41
    7. *Interference from Others* 41
    8. *Selfishness* 41
    9. *Entitlement* 42
    10. *Spiritual and Emotional Immaturity* 42
    11. *Grief and Depression* 42
    12. *Greed* 43
    13. *Shame* 43
    14. *Anger* 43
    15. *Dishonesty* 44
    16. *Worldliness* 44
    17. *Pride* 44
    18. *Disappointment* 45
    19. *Different Priorities/Value System* 45

20. Self-image 45
21. Lack of communication 46
22. Constant arguing 46
23. Lack of intimacy 47
24. In-Law Interference 47
25. Workaholism 48

Chapter 6. 25 Reasons Why Marriages Last "Till Death Do Us Part". 50

1. Pre-Marital Training 51
2. Trust 51
3. Communication 51
4. Respect 52
5. Love 52
6. Laughter 53
7. Passion 53
8. Intimacy 53
9. Conflict Resolution 54
10. Think 54
11. Express 55
12. Accept 55
13. Image 56
14. Learn 56
15. End 57
16. Enjoy 57
17. Friends 57
18. Decompress 58
19. Dates 58
20. Space 59
21. Know 59
22. Don't 60
23. Always 60

    24. Virtue 61

    25. Team 61

Chapter 7. **25 Reasons for Gratitude in 25 Marriage Years** 63

Chapter 8. **25 Lessons in 25 Marriage Years.** 69

Chapter 9. **25 Marriage Questions to Review** 72

Chapter 10. **25 Nuggets from the 25 Plus** 75

    1. *John and Wendy (Gwendolyn) Pullen* 76

    2. *Dr. Philip and Marcia Eyster* 77

    3. *President Jimmy Carter and Rosalynn Carter* 77

    4. *Rev. Dr. John and Mrs. Vivacious Veronica Ghartey* 77

    5. *Pastor John and Mrs. Lee Willis* 78

    6. *Mr. Steve and Mrs. Tracy Gibbs* 78

    7. *Rev. Joseph and Mrs. Mary Osei-Amoah* 78

    8. *Jewish liberator of Nazi camp, wife of 78 years dies hours apart.* 80

    9. *Mr. Kofi and Irene Amoa-Awuah* 81

    10. *Rev. Eric and Mrs. Felicia Amoah* 82

    11. *Rev. Dr. David and Mrs. Susan Wells* 83

    12. *Sammy and Macie Waller* 85

    13. *Frank and Thelma Hoffman* 86

    14. *James and Virginia Wilson* 87

    15. *Stewart and Sandra Brown* 88

    16. *Lewis and Marsha McGehee* 90

    17. *Carol Gee* 91

    18. *Rev. Dr. Augustine Adu-Anane and Rev. Mrs. Eleanor Adu-Anane* 92

    19. *Deacon Felix and Mrs. Charity Oppong- Kyekyeku* 93

    20. *Dr. Jacob and Mrs. Ivy Stella Otchere Al Hassan* 96

    21. *Mr. and Mrs. Emmanuel and Comfort Ayiku* 97

22. Rev. Isaac and Mrs. Tina Bonful..................................98
23. Deacon Larry Kutuadu and Mrs. Comfort Kutuadu.......99
24. Rev Christian and Mrs. Vivian Essandoh....................101
25. Rev. Professor Paul and Rev Mrs. Gladys Frimpong Manso 106

Chapter 11. 25 Marriage Jokes for Laughs 109

Chapter 12. 25 Prayers for Marriages.. 120

1. Protection...121
2. Unity..122
3. Forgiveness..123
4. Conflict..123
5. God's Presence...124
6. Intimacy..125
7. Speak To Us...126
8. Finances..127
9. Our Words...128
10. Friendships..129
11. Spiritual Growth 130
12. Legacy...131
13. Thankful..132
14. Protection..133
15. Obedience..134
16. For Our Leadership...134
17. For Divine Direction...135
18. For Our Health...136
19. Submission..137
20. Unconditional Love 138
21. Our Time...139
22. Gifts...140
23. Our Perspective...140
24. A Place Of Refuge...141

25. *Being Vulnerable With Each Other* 142

Chapter 13. 20 Honest Insights on Making It To 25 Years In Marriage **145**

1. *Love Is A Decision, Not An Emotion* 147
2. *Your Emotions Eventually Catch Up To Your Obedience* 148
3. *Don't Make Tomorrow's Decisions Based On Today's Emotions* 149
4. *Live Your Story…Not Someone Else's* 150
5. *Instagram Lies* 150
6. *Don't Put Pressure On Your Spouse That Only God Can Bear* 151
7. *You Probably Married Your Opposite* 152
8. *Counsellors Are Worth It* 153
9. *Progress Starts When You See That You're The Problem* 153
10. *Your Unspoken Assumptions Can Sink You* 154
11. *When You Agree On Values, You'll Agree A Lot More* .. 154
12. *Remember That If You Leave, You Take All Your Unresolved Problems To Your Next Relationship* 155
13. *Pray Together* 155
14. *If You are A Guy, Lead Your Marriage Spiritually* 156
15. *Go On Weekly Date Nights* 156
16. *Don't Make Your Kids The Centre Of Your Family* 157
17. *Take Personal Vacations Without The Kids* 158
18. *Take Family Vacations Every Year* 159
19. *Figure Out How To Be A Couple Again Before Your Kids Grow Up* 160
20. *Open The Gift Of Sex…It's From God* 160

Chapter 14. CONCLUSION **162**

MARRIAGE QUOTES

- ♥ To still stay married, still stay in Christ, Still stay in the Spirit and still stay humble
  —*Isaac De-Graft Takyi*

- ♥ To be truly married on earth to your wife or husband, is to be truly married to Christ
  —*Isaac De-Graft Takyi*

- ♥ Love is blind, but Marriage Restores its sight
  —*George Lichtenberg*

- ♥ The goal in marriage is not to think alike, but to think together
  —*Robert C. Dodds.*

- ♥ "A good marriage is the union of two good forgivers."
  —Ruth Bell Graham

- ♥ A successful marriage requires falling in love many times and always with the same person
  —Mignon McLaughlin

- ♥ "If I get married, I want to be very married."
  —Audrey Hepburn.

- ♥ A long lasting great and healthy marriage is the coming together of two Christ centred individuals
  —Isaac De-Graft Takyi

INTRODUCTION

Is marriage a mystery? Is marriage management? Is marriage made by the maker? Is marriage for money? Is marriage for Children? Is marriage for wealth? Is marriage for health, Is marriage for worship, Is marriage for good? Is marriage one-man one-woman affair? Is marriage a Blessing? Is marriage a curse? Is marriage of God? Is marriage of Satan? Is marriage of men. Is marriage hell? Or Is Marriage heaven?

Is your marriage a pain? Is your marriage a joy? Does your marriage need help? Can your marriage be of help? Is your marriage breaking? Is your marriage healthy, long, and stable?

We hope and trust that this book will attempt to give answers to some of the questions posed.

In this book we want to share a bit of the lessons learnt in our marriage journey of twenty-five years. We pray the insight in this book will add to end or reduce the rate of divorce in our world. The chapters touch on twenty-five reasons why marriages fail, twenty-five key quotes to add to, twenty-five scriptures that has helped us through our journey, introducing our readers to twenty-five different prayers that can be practiced. Gleaning from twenty-five marriage veterans in our lives. We conclude with some questions to reflect on without neglecting the prayer we began the book with, although it is quite a long one it is worthy to pray through as presented by Wendy Blight.

We hope and pray that this book will be a source of encouragement to every marriage couple with or without what you think should be normal in the marriage. We hope that whether your marriage is five years old, fifteen years old, twenty-five years old, thirty-five years old, forty-five years old, fifty-five years old, sixty-five years old, seventy-five years old, eighty-five years old, ninety-five years old or a hundred and five years old, you will be encouraged to keep the marriage safe, healthy, secured, long, sexy, and spiritual.

Enjoy the marriage ride.

Olivia and I like this prayer and hope it encourages you too as you pray it over your life, your spouse and children. Thanks to Wendy Blight.

1

MARRIAGE PRAYER

We praise You Father God as the Creator of every good and perfect gift, the Giver of Life, the One whose name is above all names. I recognize You as the King of Kings and Lord of Lords, as my Redeemer and Savior. You, God, are Holy and Perfect and lacking nothing, needing nothing. You are Wisdom and Knowledge. You are Healer and Restorer, Rebuilder and Rewarder.

Your Word says if anyone lacks wisdom, let him ask it of You who gives wisdom to all men liberally. Therefore, this day, I ask in faith, not doubting but believing fully. I thank You that Your Word says You know the plans You have for our marriage and our family, plans to prosper us and not to harm us, plans to give us a hope and a future. Jer. 29:11

We stand on that promise today, believing You for our marriage. Your Word says You are the Lord, the God of all mankind. There is nothing too hard for you. Jer. 32:37.

Sovereign Lord, you made the heavens and the earth by Your great power and outstretched arm. Nothing is too hard for You, not even what is going on in our marriage. No, nothing, not even this is impossible with You. Luke 18:27.

Thank You for the promise that when we seek You with all our hearts about our marriage and our family, there is no good thing that You will withhold. Psalm 34:10.

Father, you are El Roi, the God who sees our hurts, needs, and struggles. You made the way possible for redemption and healing by the blood shed by Your Son Jesus on the cross. You alone have the power to heal the hurting places in this family and in this marriage. But, I know You cannot heal until we lay aside our will, our hurts, our anger, our bitterness, our resentment, our hate, and any other issues that will keep You from being able to work.

Father forgive each of us for our parts in what brought us here today. Create in us clean and pure hearts. Show us where we have been wrong. Break our hearts and make them tender to see our faults, our selfishness, our self-centeredness and our critical spirits. Give us a spirit of humility to allow You to begin Your work in us. Eradicate all pride so You can come in and transform the brokenness and make it whole. Help us surrender our will to Yours. Help us lay on the altar anything that will get in Your way, show us those things and make them clear. Let your refining fire purify those places so we can begin to reflect You as we deal with each other. Thank You for Your promise that if we confess our sins, You are faithful and just to forgive them and purify us from all unrighteousness. We claim that promise for ourselves right now.

God, You give guidance on marriage. Specifically, You call us to certain roles. Right now, they sound impossible, but Your Word says that with you all things are possible. We pray this prayer from this day forward to release the power of Your Word and Your Spirit into this marriage. We are asking You to do as You promise—to do immeasurably more than we can ever ask or imagine. Eph. 3:20. We know and trust You will do whatever we ask in Your name because, once again, You promise this in Your Word. John 14:13-14.

You call a wife to submit to her husband as to the Lord because in Your plan of marriage the husband is the head of the wife as Christ is the head of the church. Eph. 5:22-33. As a wife, You call me to this, not to submit in a subservient way to my husband [name], but to do it as an act of submission to You. This seems impossible now because of all the circumstances and the past. But, God, I believe You alone can change my heart to submit to Your plan of marriage. Remove anything in my heart that would keep me from honoring Your Word on marriage. Remove any thoughts in my head that would contradict Your perfect will for us. You call me to respect my husband [name]. Again, there is so much pain and hurt that seems impossible to obey. But, God, I ask You to fill my mind and heart with whatever is pure, whatever is lovely, and whatever is beautiful about our marriage. Remind me of why I first fell in love.

You call a husband to love his wife as Christ loved the Church and gave Himself up for her to make her holy. Eph. 5:22-33. Father, give me a love for my wife, [name] that is like the love You have — pure, unconditional, patient, gentle, not judging, not self-seeking, not remembering wrongs but always looking for the best in her. Let me love her unselfishly. Teach me how to nurture and cherish her, to respect her. Help me to not complain or argue. Make the words of my mouth be only what is helpful and good. Give me a discerning spirit to know her needs and give me a heart to want to meet them.

God, we know You will honor our marriage only when we stay under the covering You provide in Your Word. Give us unity of heart and spirit through Your Holy Spirit. Whatever breach of honor, trust, or respect we have had in the past, we come to You together, confessing and repenting in complete humility, asking for Your forgiveness and healing. Bless us with Your richest blessing that as a couple we will together know how high and wide and deep and long is your love for us in Christ Jesus. We ask that from Your Glorious storehouses of riches You will make beautiful what has been dark and raw and hurting. Thank You that from this day forward we recommit this marriage to be rooted and established in Your deep and abiding love, the love that surpasses all knowledge. From this day forward, we pray that we will live a life worthy and live out a marriage worthy of You, Lord. Give us great endurance and patience.

Fill us with Your joy so that when we have hard days, we can look beyond the circumstances and remember the promises made in You. Keep our eyes on You and not on our faults and our circumstances. Remind us that we model You to our children. Help us to be living sacrifices to You, giving up our own desires to accomplish Your greater purposes for this family.

In whatever way our children have been hurt by this, Father, we ask You to redeem that situation. Allow them to see Your power and Your glory in all its splendor and wonder as we are transformed by the power of prayer and Your Word. Protect their tender hearts from the hurt and pain that has existed the last years. May they know Your great love for them, and may they know the assurance that our love is strong and for eternity.

Make our home one that will be built solidly on the foundation of Jesus. It will be a safe place in this world where we all feel loved and protected. Help us each to humbly submit to You and to resist Satan. We know he desires to destroy this family and gain a foothold in this home. Help us to discern his evil tactics and protect our hearts and minds from his lies, traps and deceptions. Give us Your strength and resurrection power for every spiritual battle he throws at us.

Thank you, Father, that there is hope in You, hope for a rich, wonderful future for this marriage and this family. What Satan intended for harm, you give purpose and turn into good. Cover us this day forward with Your protective hedge of safety and strength. Keep us in perfect peace. Thank You that You have begun a good work and will perfect it for Your glory.

We ask all of these things in the powerful name of JESUS. AMEN

—by Wendy Blight

2

25 MARRIAGE DEFINITIONS TO NOTE

From the Scriptures, the Jewish traditions and the state marriage definition has gone through a lot of reforms and changes but these definitions we were very intentional to look at how God want us to see it and live it out with no resentment and hatred against anyone with an opposing view.

We hope and trust that this gives you some form of conviction and encouragement to follow the God way.

1. **Marriage** generally may be defined as the state of being united as spouses in a consensual and contractual relationship recognized by law. It is the act of marrying someone, or the ceremony at which this is done.
2. **Marriage** is a powerful creator and sustainer of human and social capital for adults as well as children. It is as **important** as education when it comes to promoting the health, wealth, and well-being of adults and communities.

3. **Marriage** is a divine institution that can never be broken, even if the husband or wife legally divorce in the civil courts; as long as they are both alive, the Church considers them bound together by **God**.
4. The **Sacrament** of **Marriage** is a lasting commitment of a man and a woman to a lifelong partnership, established for the good of each other and the procreation of their children. ... Through the **sacrament** of Matrimony, the Church teaches that Jesus gives the strength and grace to live the real meaning of **marriage**.
5. **A marriage** is the relationship between two people who are married. In a good marriage, both partners work hard to solve any problems that arise.
6. **In Judaism marriage** is believed to have been instituted by God and is described as making the individual complete. Marriage involves a double ceremony, which includes the formal betrothal and wedding rites (prior to the 12th century the two were separated by as much as one year). The modern ceremony begins with the groom signing the marriage contract before a group of witnesses. He is then led to the bride's room, where he places a veil on her. This is followed by the ceremony under the huppa (a canopy that symbolizes the bridal bower), which involves the reading of the marriage contract, the seven marriage

benedictions, the groom's placing a ring on the bride's finger (in Conservative and Reform traditions the double ring ceremony has been introduced), and, in most communities, the crushing of a glass under foot. After the ceremony the couple is led into a private room for seclusion, which symbolizes the consummation of the marriage.

7. **Marriage** is the state in which men and women can live together in sexual relationship with the approval of their social group. Adultery and fornication are sexual relationships that society does not recognize as constituting marriage[1].

8. **Marriage is defined** differently, and by different entities, based on cultural, religious, and personal factors. A commonly accepted and encompassing definition of marriage is the following: a formal union and social and legal contract between two individuals that unites their lives legally, economically, and emotionally. The contractual marriage agreement usually implies that the couple has legal obligations to each other throughout their

---

[1] Thomson, J. G. S. S. (1996). Marks. In D. R. W. Wood, I. H. Marshall, A. R. Millard, J. I. Packer, & D. J. Wiseman (Eds.), New Bible dictionary (3rd ed., p. 732). Leicester, England; Downers Grove, IL: InterVarsity Press.

lives or until they decide to divorce. Being married also gives legitimacy to sexual relations within the marriage. Traditionally, marriage is often viewed as having a key role in the preservation of morals and civilization.[2]

9. **The state of** being united to a person of the opposite sex as husband or wife in a consensual and contractual relationship recognized by law (2): the state of being united to a person of the same sex in a relationship like that of a traditional marriage [same-sex marriage] b: the mutual relation or the legally or formally recognized union of two people as partners in a personal relationship (historically and in some jurisdictions specifically a union between a man and a woman). Merriam-Webster

10. **At the heart of God's** design for **marriage** is companionship and intimacy. The biblical picture of **marriage** expands into something much broader, with the husband and wife relationship illustrating the relationship between Christ and the church.

11. **Marriage** is the beginning—the beginning of the family—and is a life-long commitment. It also provides an opportunity to grow in selflessness as you serve your wife and children. **Marriage** is more than a physical union; it is

---

[2] https://www.thespruce.com/definition-of-marriage-2303011

also a spiritual and emotional union. This union mirrors the one between God and His Church.

12. **Marriage** is in its very essence a relationship between a man and a woman; and everything that marriage is derives directly from the fact that it is God's plan, God's creation. Moreover, it should be noted that it is not necessary to be a Christian in order to be able to be part of a marriage that is joined together by God. To limit being joined together by God to marriages between Christians would be to ignore the fact that marriage was not an ordinance of Christ, but of Creation, and Christ's teaching was not to change marriage in any way but to direct man's attention back to what marriage was always intended to be. One may only realize its full potential, and rise to the highest level, when it is Christian marriage Excerpt from: "Marriage and Divorce: The New Testament Teaching" by B. Ward Powers. Scribd.

13. **Marriage** is a deep and intimate relationship between a man and a woman, for the purpose of companionship, mutual help, and sexual fulfilment; it is a relationship that is to be total, exclusive, and lifelong. No person is to sunder this relationship in any way, for any reason. Marriage involves the total, exclusive, and lifelong commitment of the partners to each other. B. Ward Powers.

14. **Marriage** exists to make men and women responsible to each other and to any children that they might have. **Marriage** is thus a personal relationship that serves a public **purpose** in a political community. Mar 11, 2013

15. **Christians** believe that **marriage** is a gift from **God**, one that should not be taken for granted. It is the right atmosphere to engage in sexual relations and to build a family life. Getting **married** in a church, in front of **God**, is very **important**. A **marriage** is a public declaration of love and commitment. Marriage is God's ideal.

16. Marriage is presented in the Bible as an essential aspect of social life. It is the outcome and intention of God's creation of mankind as male and female, counterparts of each other, capable of reproduction and indeed commanded to reproduce (Gen. 1:27–28; 2:18–24). Much of the Bible is given over to regulating and teaching about marriage, especially in view of the contrast between the attitudes required of God's people toward sex and human relationships and the attitudes of surrounding peoples (e.g., Lev. 18:1–5; 1 Thess. 4:3–6).[3]

---

[3] Myers, A. C. (1987). In *The Eerdmans Bible dictionary* (p. 693). Grand Rapids, MI: Eerdmans.

17. **In all biblical teaching**, marriage is seen as being a relationship between a man and a woman. Anything else which may be true of the nature of marriage flows out of what it is first of all as a relationship.
18. **Marriage** has three purposes, or, more accurately, a single purpose which has three aspects: companionship, mutual help, and the fulfilment of the sexual natures of man and woman. It is based upon mutual commitment, and rests upon the consent of the man and the woman to its continuance.
19. **Marriage** is an ordinance of creation and is God's gift to all mankind: he made marriage for men and women, and he made men and women for marriage. But marriage is not for everyone. To some people God gives the gift of being able to be a marriage partner and needing marriage; to other people God gives the gift of being able to live a single, celibate life, without marriage. These gifts are not necessarily lifelong. Thus a person who has had, and has been called upon to exercise, the gift of celibacy may marry later in life; and a person who has been married may remain unmarried after the marriage ends (through divorce, or the death of the partner). B. Ward Powers.
20. **Marriage** is the joining into one unity of two beings who are different enriches each and extends and enlarges their

capacity to experience and enjoy life. This is so special, and so unique, that there are no analogies or illustrations that can be given which fully reflect all of it.

21. **Marriage is "complementarity".** Not that mere difference in itself is what matters: you won't get much music from a violin and a jackhammer in operation together. The similarities must be such that the two blends together, and the differences must be such that each one supplies what the other lacks and needs. And this is exactly how God has made man and woman: similar enough so that they can truly blend, and yet different in such a way that each needs the other. In a sense, each is incomplete alone, and only finds completion in unity with the other. B. Ward Powers.

22. A Christian marriage is a marriage which has been instituted and functions according to biblical principles. It is a marriage between one man and one woman (Genesis 2:24, Matthew 19:4,5). In a Christian marriage there is no room for multiple wives or husbands. Neither is a 'marriage' between two men or women a marriage according to biblical principles. A Christian marriage is a lifelong covenant between one man and one woman.

23. In the wisdom and plan of God, He instituted the marriage relationship between a man and a woman right from the beginning of human existence. It is absolutely God's

design, and never man's desire, and that is why we should endeavour to play only by His rules. Rev. Dr. John Ghartey.

24. If Gen 1:1–2:3 says much about fertility and little about marriage, Gen 2:4–25 says much about marriage and nothing about fertility. In this portion, usually called the Yahwist (J) creation account, Yahweh-Elohim created the male first. Shortly thereafter Yahweh arrived at the conclusion that it is not good for man to be by himself. It was Yahweh, not the man, who made this determination, and he turned his attention to rectifying the situation of man's aloneness. Yahweh-Elohim proceeded to make for man a helper (v 18). The Hebrew word for "helper" (*ēzer*) has particularly rich nuances throughout the OT. For example, of the twenty-one times it is used, fifteen times it refers to divine help. Most of these refer to help in times of despair or distress. As his helper, woman rescues man from his loneliness and delivers him from his solitude.[4]

25. After extracting a "rib" (?) of Adam (the only time this Hebrew word [*ṣl'*] is so translated in the OT), Yahweh-Elohim "built" it into a woman (v 22). Upon seeing her, the man exclaimed: "this one is bone of my bones and flesh

---

[4] Hamilton, V. P. (1992). Marriage: Old Testament and Ancient Near East. In D. N. Freedman (Ed.), *The Anchor Yale Bible Dictionary* (Vol. 4, p. 568). New York: Doubleday.

of my flesh" (v 23). This is more than simply an affirmation of blood ties. Both "flesh" and "bone" carry a double meaning. *Bāśār* means both "flesh/meat" and "weakness" (Isa 31:3). *'Eṣem* means both "bone" and "strength" (cf. the verbal form *'āṣamtā* in Gen 26:16 ["you are stronger than we are"]). There is in both the man and the woman the inevitable presence of the strong and the weak, and the two are therefore necessary for each other "in sickness and in health" and "in plenty and in want" (Brueggemann 1970: 534). Marriage, then, is essentially a bond of covenant loyalty.[5]

We can conclude from the definitions that, Marriage is a union between man and woman, sanctified by God as a means of maintaining family life. The idea of marriage was ordained by God in his instruction to Adam that a man should leave his father and mother, and he and his wife should be one flesh (Gen 2:24).[6]

---

[5] Hamilton, V. P. (1992). Marriage: Old Testament and Ancient Near East. In D. N. Freedman (Ed.), *The Anchor Yale Bible Dictionary* (Vol. 4, p. 568). New York: Doubleday.

[6] Elwell, W. A., & Beitzel, B. J. (1988). Marriage, Marriage Customs. In *Baker encyclopedia of the Bible* (Vol. 2, p. 1405). Grand Rapids, MI: Baker Book House.

3

25 MARRIAGE SCRIPTURES TO REFLECT ON

The word of God reveals from Genesis to Revelation that marriage is God's idea and that any married couple that engages in marriage in God's way are guaranteed success as God has prescribed it. We trust that these scriptures will be of help to you as you read, pray and meditate on them. It is essential to note that the Bible begins and ends with marriage (Gen 2:24; Rev 22:20)[7]

1. **Genesis 1:27-28:** *"So God created man in his own image, in the image of God he created him; male and female he created them. And God blessed them. And God said to them, 'Be fruitful and multiply and fill the earth and subdue it and have dominion over the fish of the sea and over the birds of*

---

[7] McWhirter, J. (2016). Marriage. In J. D. Barry, D. Bomar, D. R. Brown, R. Klippenstein, D. Mangum, C. Sinclair Wolcott, ... W. Widder (Eds.), *The Lexham Bible Dictionary*. Bellingham, WA: Lexham Press.

the heavens and over every living thing that moves on the earth.'"

2. **Genesis 2:18-25** *"The Lord God said, "It is not good for the man to be alone. I will make a helper suitable for him." Now the Lord God had formed out of the ground all the wild animals and all the birds in the sky. He brought them to the man to see what he would name them; and whatever the man called each living creature, that was its name. So the man gave names to all the livestock, the birds in the sky and all the wild animals. But for Adam no suitable helper was found. So the Lord God caused the man to fall into a deep sleep; and while he was sleeping, he took one of the man's ribs and then closed up the place with flesh. Then the Lord God made a woman from the rib he had taken out of the man, and he brought her to the man. The man said, "This is now bone of my bones and flesh of my flesh; she shall be called 'woman,' for she was taken out of man." That is why a man leaves his father and mother and is united to his wife, and they become one flesh. Adam and his wife were both naked, and they felt no shame."* (NIV)

3. **Deuteronomy 24:1-5** *"If a man marries a woman who becomes displeasing to him because he finds something indecent about her, and he writes her a certificate of divorce, gives it to her and sends her from his house, and if after she*

leaves his house she becomes the wife of another man, and her second husband dislikes her and writes her a certificate of divorce, gives it to her and sends her from his house, or if he dies, then her first husband, who divorced her, is not allowed to marry her again after she has been defiled. That would be detestable in the eyes of the Lord. Do not bring sin upon the land the Lord your God is giving you as an inheritance. If a man has recently married, he must not be sent to war or have any other duty laid on him. For one year he is to be free to stay at home and bring happiness to the wife he has married. (NIV)

4. **Proverbs 5:15-20:** "Drink water from your own cistern, running water from your own well. Should your springs overflow in the streets, your streams of water in the public squares? Let them be yours alone, never to be shared with strangers. May your fountain be blessed, and may you rejoice in the wife of your youth. A loving doe, a graceful deer— may her breasts satisfy you always, may you ever be intoxicated with her love. Why, my son, be intoxicated with another man's wife? Why embrace the bosom of a wayward woman?" (NIV)

5. **Proverbs 12:4:** *"A wife of noble character is her husband's crown, but a disgraceful wife is like decay in his bones."* (NIV)
6. **Proverbs 18:22:** *"He who finds a wife finds what is good and receives favor from the Lord."*
7. **Proverbs 19:14** *"A foolish child is a father's ruin, and a quarrelsome wife is like the constant dripping of a leaky roof. Houses and wealth are inherited from parents, but a prudent wife is from the Lord."* (NIV)
8. **Proverbs 20:6-7** *"Many a man proclaims his own steadfast love, but a faithful man who can find?"* (ESV)
9. **Proverbs 30:18-19** *""There are three things that are too amazing for me, four that I do not understand: the way of an eagle in the sky, the way of a snake on a rock, the way of a ship on the high seas, and the way of a man with a young woman."* (NIV)
10. **Proverbs 31:10-12; 25-31:** *"A wife of noble character who can find. She is worth far more than rubies. Her husband has full confidence in her and lacks nothing of value. She brings him good, not harm, all the days of her life.... She is clothed with strength and dignity; she can laugh at the days to come. She speaks with wisdom, and faithful instruction is on her tongue. She watches over the affairs of her household and does not eat the bread of idleness. Her children arise and*

call her blessed; her husband also, and he praises her: "Many women do noble things, but you surpass them all." Charm is deceptive, and beauty is fleeting; but a woman who fears the Lord is to be praised. Honor her for all that her hands have done, and let her works bring her praise at the city gate." (NIV)

11. **Ecclesiastes 4:9-12:** "Two are better than one, because they have a good return for their labor: If either of them falls down, one can help the other up. But pity anyone who falls and has no one to help them up. Also, if two lie down together, they will keep warm. But how can one keep warm alone? Though one may be overpowered, two can defend themselves. A cord of three strands is not quickly broken." (NIV)

12. **Songs of Song 8:3,6-7:** "His left arm is under my head and his right arm embraces me..... Place me like a seal over your heart, like a seal on your arm; for love is as strong as death, its jealousy unyielding as the grave. It burns like blazing fire, like a mighty flame. Many waters cannot quench love; rivers cannot sweep it away. If one were to give all the wealth of one's house for love, it would be utterly scorned." (NIV)

13. **Isaiah 54:5:** *"For your Maker is your husband, the LORD of hosts is his name; and the Holy One of Israel is your Redeemer, the God of the whole earth he is called."*

14. **Malachi 2:14-15:** *"But you say, 'Why does he not?' Because the LORD was witness between you and the wife of your youth, to whom you have been faithless, though she is your companion and your wife by covenant."*

15. **Matthew 19:3-12:** *"Some Pharisees came to him to test him. They asked, "Is it lawful for a man to divorce his wife for any and every reason?" "Haven't you read," he replied, "that at the beginning the Creator 'made them male and female,' and said, 'For this reason a man will leave his father and mother and be united to his wife, and the two will become one flesh'? So, they are no longer two, but one flesh. Therefore, what God has joined together, let no one separate." "Why then," they asked, "did Moses command that a man give his wife a certificate of divorce and send her away?" Jesus replied, "Moses permitted you to divorce your wives because your hearts were hard. But it was not this way from the beginning. I tell you that anyone who divorces his wife, except for sexual immorality, and marries another woman commits adultery." The disciples said to him, "If this is the situation between a husband and wife, it is better not to marry." Jesus replied, "Not everyone can accept this*

word, but only those to whom it has been given. For there are eunuchs who were born that way, and there are eunuchs who have been made eunuchs by others—and there are those who choose to live like eunuchs for the sake of the kingdom of heaven. The one who can accept this should accept it."" (NIV)

16. **Romans 13:8:** *"Owe no one anything, except to love each other, for the one who loves another has fulfilled the law."*

17. **Colossians 3:12-19:** *"Therefore, as God's chosen people, holy and dearly loved, clothe yourselves with compassion, kindness, humility, gentleness and patience. Bear with each other and forgive one another if any of you has a grievance against someone. Forgive as the Lord forgave you. And over all these virtues put on love, which binds them all together in perfect unity. Let the peace of Christ rule in your hearts, since as members of one body you were called to peace. And be thankful. Let the message of Christ dwell among you richly as you teach and admonish one another with all wisdom through psalms, hymns, and songs from the Spirit, singing to God with gratitude in your hearts. And whatever you do, whether in word or deed, do it all in the name of the Lord Jesus, giving thanks to God the Father through him. Wives, submit yourselves to your husbands, as is fitting in*

the Lord. Husbands, love your wives and do not be harsh with them." (NIV)

18. **Ephesians 5:22-33:** "Submit to one another out of reverence for Christ. Wives submit yourselves to your own husbands as you do to the Lord. For the husband is the head of the wife as Christ is the head of the church, his body, of which he is the Savior. Now as the church submits to Christ, so also wives should submit to their husbands in everything. Husbands, love your wives, just as Christ loved the church and gave himself up for her to make her holy, cleansing her by the washing with water through the word, and to present her to himself as a radiant church, without stain or wrinkle or any other blemish, but holy and blameless. In this same way, husband's ought to love their wives as their own bodies. He who loves his wife loves himself. After all, no one ever hated their own body, but they feed and care for their body, just as Christ does the church— for we are members of his body. "For this reason, a man will leave his father and mother and be united to his wife, and the two will become one flesh." This is a profound mystery—but I am talking about Christ and the church. However, each one of you also must love his wife as he loves himself, and the wife must respect her husband." (NIV)

19. **Ephesians 4:1-3:** *"As a prisoner for the Lord, then, I urge you to live a life worthy of the calling you have received. Be completely humble and gentle; be patient, bearing with one another in love. Make every effort to keep the unity of the Spirit through the bond of peace."* (NIV)

20. **1 Corinthians 7:1-16:** *"Now for the matters you wrote about: "It is good for a man not to have sexual relations with a woman." But since sexual immorality is occurring, each man should have sexual relations with his own wife, and each woman with her own husband. The husband should fulfill his marital duty to his wife, and likewise the wife to her husband. The wife does not have authority over her own body but yields it to her husband. In the same way, the husband does not have authority over his own body but yields it to his wife. Do not deprive each other except perhaps by mutual consent and for a time, so that you may devote yourselves to prayer. Then come together again so that Satan will not tempt you because of your lack of self-control. I say this as a concession, not as a command. I wish that all of you were as I am. But each of you has your own gift from God; one has this gift, another has that. Now to the unmarried and the widows I say: It is good for them to stay unmarried, as I do. But if they cannot control themselves,*

they should marry, for it is better to marry than to burn with passion. To the married I give this command (not I, but the Lord): A wife must not separate from her husband. But if she does, she must remain unmarried or else be reconciled to her husband. And a husband must not divorce his wife. To the rest I say this (I, not the Lord): If any brother has a wife who is not a believer and she is willing to live with him, he must not divorce her. And if a woman has a husband who is not a believer and he is willing to live with her; she must not divorce him. For the unbelieving husband has been sanctified through his wife, and the unbelieving wife has been sanctified through her believing husband. Otherwise your children would be unclean, but as it is, they are holy. But if the unbeliever leaves, let it be so. The brother or the sister is not bound in such circumstances; God has called us to live in peace. How do you know, wife, whether you will save your husband? Or, how do you know, husband, whether you will save your wife?" (NIV)

21. **1 Corinthians 13:1-3:** *"If I speak in the tongues of men or of angels, but do not have love, I am only a resounding gong or a clanging cymbal. If I have the gift of prophecy and can fathom all mysteries and all knowledge, and if I have a faith that can move mountains, but do not have love, I am nothing. If I give all I possess to the poor and give over my*

body to hardship that I may boast, but do not have love, I gain nothing." (NIV)

22. **1 Corinthians 13:4-12:** "Love is patient, love is kind. It does not envy, it does not boast, it is not proud. It does not dishonor others, it is not self-seeking, it is not easily angered, it keeps no record of wrongs. Love does not delight in evil but rejoices with the truth. It always protects, always trusts, always hopes, always perseveres. Love never fails. But where there are prophecies, they will cease; where there are tongues, they will be stilled; where there is knowledge, it will pass away. For we know in part and we prophesy in part, but when completeness comes, what is in part disappears. When I was a child, I talked like a child, I thought like a child, I reasoned like a child. When I became a man, I put the ways of childhood behind me. For now, we see only a reflection as in a mirror; then we shall see face to face. Now I know in part; then I shall know fully, even as I am fully known." (NIV)

23. **Hebrews 13:4-8:** "Marriage should be honored by all, and the marriage bed kept pure, for God will judge the adulterer and all the sexually immoral. Keep your lives free from the love of money and be content with what you have, because God has said, "Never will I leave you; never will I forsake

you." So, we say with confidence, "The Lord is my helper; I will not be afraid. What can mere mortals do to me?" Remember your leaders, who spoke the word of God to you. Consider the outcome of their way of life and imitate their faith. Jesus Christ is the same yesterday and today and forever." (NIV)

24. **1 Peter 3:7:** "In the same way, you husbands must give honor to your wives. Treat your wife with understanding as you live together. She may be weaker than you are, but she is your equal partner in God's gift of new life. Treat her as you should so your prayers will not be hindered."

25. **Revelation 19:6-9:** [6] Then I heard what seemed to be the voice of a great multitude, like the roar of many waters and like the sound of mighty peals of thunder, crying out,
"Hallelujah!
For the Lord our God
    the Almighty reigns.
[7] Let us rejoice and exult
    and give him the glory,
for the marriage of the Lamb has come,
    and his Bride has made herself ready;
[8] it was granted her to clothe herself
    with fine linen, bright and pure"—

for the fine linen is the righteous deeds of the saints.

⁹ And the angel said[a] to me, "Write this: Blessed are those who are invited to the marriage supper of the Lamb." And he said to me, "These are the true words of God." (ESV)

Our conviction is that when you learn to believe, trust and obey the word of God in your marriage life, the marriage will not only last for a long time but will also become healthy, strong and enjoyable too. It will benefit the community and bring glory to God.

4

25 MARRIAGE QUOTES TO ADD TO

Many people based on their experiences with marriage have put their lessons in life in the form of quotes for future generations. We believe that these beautiful and wonderful quotes when genuinely reflected upon will energize your marriage into degrees of celebration.

1. "It is not a lack of love, but a lack of friendship that makes unhappy marriages."—*Friedrich Nietzsche*
2. "So, it's not gonna be easy. It's going to be really hard; we're gonna have to work at this everyday, but I want to do that because I want you. I want all of you, forever, everyday. You and me... everyday."—*Nicholas Sparks*
3. "I don't want to be married just to be married. I can't think of anything lonelier than spending the rest of my life with someone I can't talk to, or worse, someone I can't be silent with." — *Mary Ann Shaffer, The Guernsey Literary and Potato Peel Pie*

4. "No woman wants to be in submission to a man who isn't in submission to God!"—*T. D. Jakes*

5. "If I get married, I want to be very married."—*Audrey Hepburn*

6. "A great marriage is not when the 'perfect couple' comes together. It is when an imperfect couple learns to enjoy their differences." —*Dave Meurer*

7. "To be loved but not known is comforting but superficial. To be known and not loved is our greatest fear. But to be fully known and truly loved is, well, a lot like being loved by God. It is what we need more than anything. It liberates us from pretense, humbles us out of our self-righteousness, and fortifies us for any difficulty life can throw at us."—*Timothy Keller, The Meaning of Marriage: Facing the Complexities of Commitment with the Wisdom of God*

8. "Within this Christian vision of marriage, here's what it means to fall in love. It is to look at another person and get a glimpse of what God is creating, and to say, "I see who God is making you, and it excites me! I want to be part of that. I want to partner with you and God in the journey you are taking to his throne. And when we get there, I will look at your magnificence and say, 'I always knew you could be

like this. I got glimpses of it on earth, but now look at you!"
—*Timothy Keller*

9. "There is nothing more admirable than when two people who see eye to eye keep house as man and wife, confounding their enemies and delighting their friends."
—*Homer, The Odyssey*

10. "The remedy for most marital stress is not in divorce. It is in repentance and forgiveness, in sincere expressions of charity and service. It is not in separation. It is in simple integrity that leads a man and a woman to square up their shoulders and meet their obligations. It is found in the Golden Rule, a time-honored principle that should first and foremost find expression in marriage." —*Gordon B. Hinckley, Standing for Something: 10 Neglected Virtues That Will Heal Our Hearts and Homes*

11. "By all means marry; if you get a good wife, you'll become happy; if you get a bad one, you'll become a philosopher."
—*Socrates*

12. "After all these years, I see that I was mistaken about Eve in the beginning; it is better to live outside the Garden with her than inside it without her."—*Mark Twain, Diaries of Adam & Eve aged as "marriage" Showing 91-120 of 5,561*

13. "Love is a commitment that will be tested in the most vulnerable areas of spirituality, a commitment that will

force you to make some very difficult choices. It is a commitment that demands that you deal with your lust, your greed, your pride, your power, your desire to control, your temper, your patience, and every area of temptation that the Bible clearly talks about. It demands the quality of commitment that Jesus demonstrates in His relationship to us."—*Ravi Zacharias, I, Isaac, Take Thee, Rebekah: Moving from Romance to Lasting Love*

14. "To keep your marriage brimming, with love in the wedding cup, whenever you're wrong, admit it; whenever you're right, shut up." —*Ogden Nash*

15. "In a word, live together in the forgiveness of your sins, for without it no human fellowship, least of all a marriage, can survive. Don't insist on your rights, don't blame each other, don't judge or condemn each other, don't find fault with each other, but accept each other as you are, and forgive each other every day from the bottom of your hearts…" —*Dietrich Bonhoeffer, Letters and Papers from Prison*

16. "Patience gives your spouse permission to be human. It understands that everyone fails. When a mistake is made, it chooses to give them more time that they deserve to correct it. It gives you the ability to hold on during the

rough times in your relationship rather than bailing out under the pressure." —*Stephen Kendrick, The Love Dare*

17. "Encouragement requires empathy and seeing the world from your spouse's perspective. We must first learn what is important to our spouse. Only then can we give encouragement. With verbal encouragement, we are trying to communicate, "I know. I care. I am with you. How can I help?" We are trying to show that we believe in him and in his abilities. We are giving credit and praise."—*Gary Chapman, The Five Love Languages: How to Express Heartfelt Commitment to Your Mate*

18. "Daughter! Get you an honest Man for a Husband and keep him honest. No matter whether he is rich, provided he be independent. Regard the Honour and moral Character of the Man more than all other Circumstances. Think of no other Greatness but that of the soul, no other Riches but those of the Heart. An honest, Sensible humane Man, above all the Littlenesses of Vanity, and Extravagances of Imagination, labouring to do good rather than be rich, to be useful rather than make a show, living in a modest Simplicity clearly within his Means and free from Debts or Obligations, is really the most respectable Man in Society, makes himself and all about him the most

happy."—*John Adams, Letters of John Adams, Addressed to His Wife*

19. "The heart is like a woman, and the head is like a man, and although man is the head of woman, woman is the heart of man, and she turns man's head because she turns his heart."—*Peter Kreeft, Jesus-Shock*

20. "If there is such a thing as a good marriage, it is because it resembles friendship rather than love."—*Michel de Montaigne*

21. "Become the kind of person the kind of person you would like to marry would like to marry."—*Douglas Wilson*

22. "Marrying means to halve one's rights and double one's duties"—*Arthur Schopenhauer*

23. "Marriage isn't a love affair. It isn't even a honeymoon. It's a job. A long hard job, at which both partners have to work, harder than they've worked at anything in their lives before. If it's a good marriage, it changes, it evolves, but it does on getting better. I've seen it with my own mother and father. But a bad marriage can dissolve in a welter of resentment and acrimony. I've seen that, too, in my own miserable and disastrous attempt at making another person happy. And it's never one person's fault. It's the sum total of a thousand little irritations, disagreements, idiotic details that in a sound alliance would simply be

disregarded or forgotten in the healing act of making love. Divorce isn't a cure, it's a surgical operation, even if there are no children to consider."—*Rosamunde Pilcher, Wild Mountain Thyme*

24. "They say all marriages are made in heaven, but so are thunder and lightning."—*Clint Eastwood*

25. "The Puritan ethic of marriage was first to look not for a partner whom you do love passionately at this moment but rather for one whom you can love steadily as your best friend for life, then to proceed with God's help to do just that."—*J.I. Packer, Worldly Saints: The Puritans as They Really Were*

What do you think about the quotes? And what do you think will be your best marriage quote?

5

25 REASONS WHY MARRIAGES FAIL

It's a pretty simple concept -- fall in love and share your life together. Our great grandparents did it, our grandparents followed suit, and for many of us, our parents did it as well. Why the hell can't we? Our generation just isn't equipped to handle marriages -- and here's why.

—Anthony D'Ambrosio, Contributor

A healthy society is a product of healthy families with healthy children growing up in a healthy marriage. Therefore, the numbers of studies on marriage and family issues are increasing. The divorce rate in many first world countries (for example, Canada and U.S.) is extremely high. Between 2001 and 2005, 353,106 marriages ended in divorce in Canada (Statistics Canada 2008). In the U.S, 2,131,000 couples got married in 2012 and 851,000 marriages ended in divorce in the same year.

Marriages in the world, fail for many reasons and often from a combination of reasons. Unaddressed personal and spiritual issues will affect both partners, even if one is unaware or innocent. While there is little difference between Christian and non-Christian marital woes, a Christ-follower has the power to recognize issues in the light of God's Word and experience the transforming power of His Spirit. Marital bliss is fictional, but marital happiness *can* be a reality. As you read through these factors for failure you can look for their opposites and that will help you know how marriages succeed in spite of the challenges, difficulties, struggles and the pain that happens in marriages while on earth.

1. *Unforgiving Spirit*

Learn to extend <u>forgiveness</u> because it's critical to harmony. Instead of obsessing about how you've been wronged, treat your spouse how God treats you. *"Bear with each other and forgive whatever grievances you may have against one another. Forgive as the Lord forgave you."* (<u>Colossians 3:13</u>)

2. Financial Pressure

Money makes people funny, or so the saying goes, and it's true. Why is divorce so common due to financial incompatibility? According to several studies and divorce statistics, a "final straw" reason for divorce is a lack of financial compatibility and money mistakes in marriage. Everything from different spending habits and financial goals to one spouse making considerably more money than the other, causing a power struggle can strain a marriage to the breaking point. "Money really touches everything. It impacts people's lives," said Emmet Burns, brand marketing director for SunTrust. Clearly, money and stress do seem to go hand in hand for many couples. Financial troubles can be categorized as one of the biggest causes of divorce, following infidelity, the number one reason for divorce. Don't spend your life trying to earn more and spend more, or you will enslave yourself to a life of dissatisfaction, materialism, and endless stress. *"For the love of money is the root of all kinds of evil. Some people, eager for money, have wandered from the faith and pierced themselves through with many griefs."* (1 Timothy 6:10)

3. Infidelity

Is sex almost absent in your marriage? Watch it. Lust always leads to infidelity of the heart, mind, and body. No sexual experience outside of marriage is okay. God will never lead you to fall in love with someone other than your spouse. *"You shall not commit adultery."* (Exodus 20:14)

4. Insecurity and Worry

Take your eyes off the world and its illusion of happiness; you will never find peace from anyone or anything the world offers you. Trust in the Lord. *"But seek first the kingdom of God and his righteousness, and all these things will be given to you as well. Therefore, do not worry about tomorrow."* (Matthew 6:32-33)

5. Secret Sins

If you hide a sinful fantasy or habit, it will grow stronger; pretending something doesn't exist or isn't wrong gives it greater power over your life. *"You have set our iniquities before you, our secret sins in the light of your presence."* (Psalm 90:8)

6. Parenting Differences

The Bible is the best parenting source available; seek to follow Christ and point your kids toward Christ, and parenting details will fall into place. *"Do not exasperate your children; instead, bring them up in the nurture and admonition of the Lord."* (Ephesians 6:4)

7. Interference from Others

Dysfunctional or controlling relatives and friends will put tremendous pressure on your family unit; seek God's wisdom and perspective about how to handle your decisions. Then draw necessary boundaries with everyone outside God's will for your life. *"Respect one another out of reverence for Christ."* (Ephesians 5:21)

8. Selfishness

We all look out for ourselves, especially when someone challenges our desires. Begin considering your spouse's perspective first; winning an argument only weakens your marriage. *"Do nothing out of selfish ambition or vain conceit. Rather, in humility, value others above yourselves."* (Philippians 2:23)

9. Entitlement

Self-pity, disillusionment, and frustration come from an "I-deserve-this" attitude. Watch for these feelings—the core problem is self-worship. *"You covet but you cannot get what you want, so you quarrel and fight. You do not have because you do not ask God. When you ask, you do not receive because you ask with wrong motives, that you may spend what you get on your pleasures."* (James 4:2-3)

10. Spiritual and Emotional Immaturity

Maturity takes a lifetime, so give your spouse room to grow without ridiculing or reprimanding him/her for immaturity. Surround your marriage with godly, mature role models. *"I press on toward the goal to win the prize for which God has called me in Christ Jesus. All of us who are mature should take such a view of things."* (Philippians 3:14-15)

11. Grief and Depression

Everyone goes through periods of grief and sadness; be supportive and understanding when your spouse is sad, by gently guiding him/her toward help. *"Be merciful to me, Lord, for I am in distress;*

my eyes grow weak with sorrow, my soul and body with grief."* (Psalm 31:9)

12. Greed

You were created to be satisfied only in God's presence. Don't feed greed because the things you want will not satisfy you. *"No one can serve two masters. Either you will hate the one and love the other, or you will be devoted to one and despise the other."* (Luke 16:13)

13. Shame

God's Spirit convicts us when we sin; He doesn't shame us for our mistakes. Embrace that fact that Jesus' grace will set you free from the shame you feel. *"I live in disgrace all day long and my face is covered with shame."* (Psalm 44:15)

14. Anger

If you have a short fuse, you need to find out why and stop making excuses. Get help to overcome this destructive and addictive habit. *"Let all bitterness, and wrath, and anger, and clamor, and evil speaking, be put away from you, with all malice."* (Ephesians 4:31)

15. Dishonesty

Never lie, mislead, or deceive your spouse; don't keep secrets because it will drive a wedge between you. Plus, one falsehood always births another one. *"Do not lie to each other."* (Colossians 3:9)

16. Worldliness

When your hearts pines for recognition, wealth, and beauty, you will believe that your worth is attached to who you are and what you do; and the more you doubt your worth, the more you will find your spouse to be unsatisfactory. *"Teaching us, that denying all ungodliness and worldly lusts, we should live soberly, righteously, and godly in this present world."* (Titus 2:12)

17. Pride

Here lies the root of all conflict, insecurities, and sin. So instead of thinking about yourself, spend your energy and love by giving your spouse grace and love. *"Where there is strife, there is pride, but wisdom is found with those who take advice."* (Proverbs 13:10)

18. Disappointment

When hard times hit, you might feel that your spouse has not done enough to make you happy. Take a look at where you place your hope; if it's not God, you will continually struggle with disappointment. Start praising God for all His provision, and your disappointment will vanish. *"Why are you downcast, O my soul? Why so disturbed within me? Put your hope in God, for I will yet praise him, my Savior and my God."* (Psalm 42:5)

19. Different Priorities/Value System

You and your spouse may have lived by opposite standards, which can cause contention and frustration. Try to remember that God holds you accountable for *your* actions; live your life and don't focus on what your spouse is doing or not doing. *"How can a young person stay on a path to purity? By living according to your word. I seek you with all my heart; do not let me stray from your commands."* (Psalm 119:10-11)

20. Self-image

If you suffer from low self-esteem, the solution is not to love yourself more—it's to love God and thank Him for His ongoing work in your life. Let God transform you into His image; embrace *your* process, instead of comparing yourself to others. *"I praise you because I am fearfully and wonderfully made; your works are wonderful, I know that full well."* (Psalm 139:14)

21. Lack of communication

Communication is crucial in marriage and not being able to communicate effectively quickly leads to resentment and frustration for both, impacting all aspects of a marriage. On the other hand, good communication is the foundation of a strong marriage. Yelling at your spouse, not talking enough throughout the day, making nasty comments to express yourself are all unhealthy methods of communication that need to be ditched in a marriage. Poor communication is one of the biggest reasons for divorce. Practicing mindful communication, to change age-old marriage mistakes, can be hard but it's well worth the effort to improve and save your relationship.

22. Constant arguing

From bickering about chores to arguing about the kids; incessant arguing kills many relationships. Couples who seem to keep having the same argument over again often do so because they feel they're not being heard or appreciated. Many find it hard to see the other person's point of view, which leads to a lot of arguments without ever coming to a resolution, which can ultimately be a cause of divorce.

23. Lack of intimacy

Not feeling connected to your partner can quickly ruin a marriage because it leaves couples feeling as though they're living with a stranger or more like roommates than spouses. This can be from a lack of physical or emotional intimacy and isn't always about sex. If you are constantly giving your spouse the cold shoulder, then know that over time it can become the ground for divorce. Ignoring your partner's sexual needs is being called the number one cause of divorce in recent times. Making your relationship intimate and special is the responsibility of both partners. Practice little acts of kindness, appreciation and enjoy physical intimacy as much as possible to sweeten your relationship.

24. In-Law Interference

If your in-laws interfere in every conversation, decision and lifestyle choice that you and your partner make, it can end up making to the list of valid reasons for divorce. It is annoying to have somebody telling you, no matter how experienced and wise they are, on how to interact, what to do with your life and where and when to go. An overbearing, looming presence of in-laws in a couple's married life is one of the causes of divorce today. *That is why a man leaves his father and mother and is united to his wife, and they become one flesh.* Genesis 2:24

25. Workaholism

It is hard to have a happy marriage with someone who is never around. If one spouse is incapable of forming a healthy work-life balance, it takes a toll on the marriage. The emotional intimacy that is healthy and necessary in a functioning marriage is difficult to create or maintain when the other spouse is always at work. Workaholism can also lead to resentment between spouses. The person who is always working may blame their spouse for "making" them work such long hours. The workaholic may see their spouse as living an overly extravagant lifestyle or not "pulling their weight." Conversely, the spouse who is working more normal hours may resent having to take care of the house more or less by themselves. They may feel that it is not right that they come home from work and still have to handle all of the household duties because their spouse cannot be bothered to come home on time. Regardless of where a workaholic marriage falls, problems can start building up quickly. *Unless the* LORD *builds the house, those who build it labor in vain. Unless the* LORD *watches over the city, the watchman stays awake in vain. It is in vain that you rise up early and go late to rest, eating the bread of anxious toil; for he gives to his beloved sleep.* (Psalm 127:1-2)

It is important to understand that you are your number one enemy when it comes to the health and longevity of your marriage. You have to lead yourself well in the marriage and the marriage will out last you. Personal growth and development discipline in an individual's life is not an option if the desires is for a long-lasting and healthy marriage. Your marriage will never fail if you learn to grow you. So please grow you and let the Lord change your spouse.

6

25 REASONS WHY MARRIAGES LAST "TILL DEATH DO US PART"

"I have waited for this opportunity for more than half a century, to repeat to you once again my vow of eternal fidelity and everlasting love"—Gabriel Garcia Marquez

"Do not make tomorrow's decisions based on today's emotions. Decide not to decide"—Unknown

It is common knowledge that 50 percent of all Canada and U.S. marriages end in divorce, right? Wrong. In reality, since 1980, divorce rates have been declining steadily. That means, contrary to popular belief, more marriages last than fail. So how are these couples building relationships that stand the test of time? Easy. They are ensuring their marriages are brimming with the following:

1. Pre-Marital Training

Did you know couples are 30 percent less likely to get a divorce if they get some sort of premarital training? According to Dr. Greg Smalley of *The Focus on the Family,"* there is no profession, skill and talent that do not require some form of training or orientation. Get some training before you marry.

2. Trust

Trust is the foundation of any healthy marriage. Without it, a couple will never be able to enjoy all of a marriage's intangible benefits wholly. Trust is not easily come by, either. Partners earn trust little by little as they prove to one another they are worthy of receiving it, which is why love is sometimes independent of trust. We can love a partner but not necessarily trust them. But when we trust a partner, loving them becomes much easier.

3. Communication

Another key to building but, more importantly, maintaining a healthy relationship is communication. It is essential for couples to confront each other and keep each other informed when issues arise so they can address and work through them. Without effectively communicating, a couple's problems will usually fester and eventually get out of hand, possibly leading them to a divorce.

4. Respect

Without mutual respect, a marriage will fail. Having respect for a partner means listening to that person's point of view and being mindful of how they deliver criticism. To get respect, it is necessary to first give it.

5. Love

Love is not enough to keep a marriage intact, but it is necessary for keeping it strong, healthy, and enjoyable. If a couple is not in love, over time, they will find themselves lacing in the drive they need to make their marriage work. Think of love like fuel; without it, a relationship will eventually break down and stop moving. Being in a loveless marriage is no fun.

6. Laughter

What is enjoyable is laughing with your partner, even during difficult times. The ability to laugh means being able to step outside ourselves and recognize the imperfect creatures we are, just like our partner. It also means having the capacity to take a break from any troubles that can bring us down and recharge our batteries.

7. Passion

Infused through all good marriages is passion. Having passion means, even after decades of being together, looking past the flaws that have come with age and still want to make out with each other like teenagers. All kidding aside, it means engaging in a healthy sex life, as well as touching in more than a platonic way.

8. Intimacy

What ultimately arises when all of the above factors are in place is intimacy, or the feeling of closeness shared when a couple's marriage is satisfying. A couple who is intimate enjoys a physical, emotion, and sexual bond that is unique to only them. A couple who is intimate knows they can depend on each other through bad days as well as enjoy each other during good ones, which is truly what it means to live happily ever after.

9. Conflict Resolution

It might seem counterintuitive, but your marriage *needs* conflict to flourish. Healthy conflict is the doorway into the deepest levels of intimacy and connection in your relationship. You have the opportunity to use conflict—those times when you're hurt, annoyed, frustrated, wounded, confused, angry and discouraged with each other—to grow closer together. Leverage conflict to your advantage in your marriage.

10. Think

Let your partner know you're thinking about them throughout the day. If you want your partner to feel both desirable and desired, make sure you're letting them know just how often they're on your mind. "Let your partner know you are thinking about them and putting them first in your mind," suggests Beverly B. Palmer, PhD, a professor of psychology, clinical psychologist, and author who has been married for 50 years. So, check on them during the day, text, WhatsApp, email, get them a gift, and make a call. Just make sure, your spouse know that you are thinking about them.

11. *Express*

Let them express their feelings first. Instead of always letting your partner know exactly how you're feeling first, make space for them to express themselves before you start sharing. "Understand your partner's point of view and let your partner know that," says Palmer. "After that, you can express yours."

12. *Accept*

Accept your partner for who they are. Houses are fixer-uppers, but viewing your spouse that way is a recipe for disaster. "Accept your partner just for who they are. Don't try to change them," Palmer recommends. After all, people can only change if *they* want to. "Just accept their strengths and weaknesses that make them unique and that you love them for that."

13. Image

Imagine what your life would really be like without them? Just because your relationship gets rocky from time to time doesn't mean you and your spouse aren't a good match—just try imagining life without them and you'll realize how important they are to you. "Sometimes, when I have a couple in counseling who are either antagonistic toward one another or apathetic, I tell them: 'Think about that you may not have tomorrow with the one you love,'" says Palmer. "'What would you wish you had said or done today that would have made a difference?

14. Learn

Learn how to compromise. Listen, all couples fight. But half the battle of marriage is knowing which fights to pick and which ones you should meet your spouse on halfway. "We compromise," says Anna Pallante, who has been married to her husband Aniello for 58 years. "When you love each other, you commit to make the bumpy road of life smoother together. When you do that each day, you put the love and each other first, instead of yourself. That keeps things peaceful."

15. End

End the night on a positive note. Before you turn in for the evening, make sure you and your spouse are on the same page about the disagreements you had earlier in the day. "Don't go to bed angry," says Bert. Do not let the sun set on your anger.

16. Enjoy

Enjoy one another's company. With work, social commitments, and other family members competing for your time, it may be difficult to allocate one-on-one time with your spouse. But making a point to do so—and enjoying it—can make your relationship stronger in the long run. "One of the very most important things is enjoying doing things together," says Tom Wilbur, who has been married for 49 years.

17. Friends

Maintain the friendship in your relationship. As your relationship progresses, don't forget to maintain your friendship along with the romantic side of your relationship. "We have always been able to spend a great deal of time together and a true friendship was easily formed," says Barbara Adoff, who has been married to her husband Bill for 47 years. "Best friends are there for each other, support each other, and like to have fun together. I often tell my hubby I feel like we're having one very long sleepover."

18. Decompress

Decompress together. Self-care is important—and performing those restorative acts with your partner can often make your relationship stronger along the way. "We manage to get into our hot tub most days and this relaxing down time is a treat," says Barbara. "Treats are being good to yourself and to each other."

19. Dates

Make everything a date. Want to keep your marriage strong? Take any opportunity to spend time together. "Just going to the grocery store together should be treated like a date," says Barbara's husband, Bill.

20. Space

Don't be afraid to give each other space. Space doesn't have to be a bad thing. Just because you want to spend time away from your partner doesn't mean you love or cherish them any less. "I credit still being married to living in a big house," Maureen McEwan, who's been married to her husband Tom for more than 50 years, told Good Housekeeping. "I need space. I need to know that I can be by myself and [have room to be] artistic."

21. Know

Know that the grass is not always greener. Many people end up unhappy in their marriage because they wonder, "What if there's someone better out there for me?" or "What if this is not the right path for me?" But, most of the time, the answers to those questions are: "There isn't," and "It is." "My grandkids won't settle down because they think the grass is greener," Sheldon Y., who's been married for 50 years, told Elite Daily. "I met my wife and asked her to marry me three days later. When you know someone is right for you, settle down with them and don't let them go. The grass is never greener than love you foster over many years."

22. Don't

Don't be afraid to seek professional help. Seeking outside help is still a bit taboo in some circles where people assume marriage counseling insinuates their relationship is weak. However, it's actually quite the opposite. "I'm not Cinderella, and he's not Prince Charming," Sherri Sugarman, who's been married to her husband Charlie for more than 50 years, told *Good Housekeeping*. "Glitches along the way are normal because it's hard to live together all these years. We went to a marriage counselor at one point because we were going in different directions and needed professional help. You always have to keep working on the relationship."

23. Always

Always kiss each other goodnight. The world is full of surprises, and not all of them good, so make the most of every moment with your partner—especially at the end of the day. "Always kiss each other goodnight because you never know what tomorrow may bring," Joyce Smith Speares, who's been married to Benny DeWitt for more than 60 years, told *Southern Living*.

24. Virtue

Understand that patience *is* a virtue. It's true. If you hope for anything out of your spouse, hope for patience. "Patience has made our marriage resilient, and has been one of the most important reasons that we are still living happily ever after, enjoying our gold years," Ann Yedowitz, who has been married to her husband Joe for more than 50 years, told Southern Living.

25. Team

And know that you're a team, no matter what. The secret to a happy, loving marriage? Knowing that you're in it together, as a team, no matter what either of you face individually. Once you're married, everything should be faced together. "I know Alan is there for me, "Evelyn Brier told *Good Housekeeping* about her husband of more than 50 years. "I was sick with breast cancer [eight] years ago, and he was right there. It was important, and satisfying, to know that there's someone who genuinely cares about my wellbeing. That's what loves does."

Trust that you know your marriage can last and must last, keep on keeping on. Marry each other, please marry each other very well. Don't underestimate the importance of friendship, fun and forgiveness.

> "So, when bills pile up, communication breaks down and you're just plain irritated with your husband or wife, Gary Thomas offers these reminders to help ease the tension: God created marriage as a loyal partnership between one man and one woman, Marriage is the firmest foundation for building a family, God designed sexual expression to help married couples build intimacy, and Marriage mirrors God's covenant relationship with His people."

7

25 REASONS FOR GRATITUDE IN 25 MARRIAGE YEARS

We thank God, and in emulating Paul in Romans chapter 16, we will love to really take this chapter to express our gratitude to God for His love and provision for us particularly for the men and women, or better still sons and daughters He brought our way and continues to bring to help us be and remain matured in Him and to fulfill His plan and purposes for our lives. We trust that you will not focus on what you do not have but count your blessing, as the song writer sang.

Therefore, join us to thank God:

1. For the parents He gave us; Mr. Isaac Kwamina De-Graft Takyi and Auntie Alberta Agyapong. Mr. Emmanuel George Ofori and Madam Esther Tenkorang.
2. For the villages and towns in which we were born. Agona Odoben in the Central Region and Accra in the Greater Accra Region of Ghana.

3. For the siblings He gave us: Yaw, Charles, Ivy, Medirose, Chezrie, Margaret, Vida, Evelyn, Irene and Samuel.
4. For the extended families of Grand parents, Aunties, Uncles, Nephews, Cousins we are very grateful.
5. For the Salvation we have in Christ. The faith we have in Christ and the Calling we have to serve Christ in the world.
6. For the schools and classmates, we have: Kotobabi 1 and 11, Swedru Secondary school, Mfantsipim School, Amanokrom Presby School, and Okuapeman Secondary School.
7. For the University of Ghana where we both studied and for the friendships that brought us together, Mrs. Joana Ndur-Osei, you shall be remembered.
8. For the great friends and colleagues from the Assemblies of God Campus Ministry and Presby-Methodist Students Union, your presence and encouragement did the trick.
9. For the Denominations that we are a part of, The Assemblies of God Church, The Presbyterian Church of Ghana, and now The Pentecostal Assemblies of Canada.
10. The churches that the Lord used to save us-Ebenezer Assemblies of God church, Kotobabi, under the late Rev. Emmanuel Adri who ensured that I was discipled, baptised in water and in the Holy Spirit. Kanda Presbyterian Church under the leadership of Rev. J.H. Ofosuhene.

11. For the secondary schools we were a part of that had Scripture union which was undeniably a great ground for our spiritual growth and maturity, all the patrons and travel secretaries we are very grateful.
12. For the first church we were a part of to be planted, Deliverance Assemblies of God church family, thanks for providing for my school when I was in middle school going to secondary.
13. For the second church that ensured that I was supported to answer the call of God upon my life, Revival Restoration Center Assemblies of God, Apostle Dr. Nkrumah and Rev. Mrs. Nkrumah and the board, not forgetting the late Rev Robert Alifo.
14. For the Brethren and Sistheren that I grew up with in the church: Rev. Ernest Birikorang, Rev. Eric Owusu Nortey, Rev. John Kofi Amissah, Mr. David Dorkenu, Mr. Godwin Amoo, Lawyer Nii Laryea, Mrs. Juliana Riverson.
15. For the leadership team and members, I had as an AGCM president at Legon—just a few that I have around in Canada now; Dr. Jonell Agyei-Sakyi, Mrs. Joana Ndur-Osei, Dr. Peter Arthur, and Dr. Godwin Ashiabi.
16. For the room mates I had in sixth form at Mfantsipim and Legon, Mr Giles Apeadu-Mensah (C-Snake), and Rev Dr.

Willie Lamptey. These are all seasoned believers; to them am grateful.

17. For the board, leaders and members of Lighthouse Assemblies of God, Toronto Canada we are very thankful for offering us the opportunity to Pastor in Canada.
18. For the Board, leaders and members of Living Word Assemblies of God, Toronto Canada for your decision to have us continue with God's work after the great work done by Rev and Mrs. Osei-Amoah.
19. For the Western Ontario District family that we serve with, particularly Rev. Lorry Gibbons the Superintendent, and his team, not forgetting my good friend Rev. Tom and Kathy Quinn, we say thank you for your love for us.
20. For all the children that have been named after us in the world we say God grant you good health to grow up to do that which we could not do.
21. For the children that lived with us Kyeiwa, Adwoa, Kesewa, Michael and Ben, we say thank you for granting us the experience of parenting.
22. For the sons and daughters we have gotten when we were in Ghana and when we came to Canada, namely, Brothers: Kwamevie, Tony Mensah, Caesar Mensah, Joe Kaba, Prince Boakye, late Asare; and sisters; Jacqueline Adu-Attoh, Akos Adu-Attoh, Mrs. Mary Yeboah, Serwah and Akoto, Ernest

Darko, Kofi Kodua, Randy Ekwam, Veronica Dickson, Mrs. Belinda Osei, Abigail Ansah-Dei, Solomon and Gifty, Comfort and Eleanor Oduro-Yeboah, Evelyn Aheto (Mrs. Quaigrene), Mrs. Evelyn Amoo, Stella Mensah, Eva, Dora Antwi, the Marfo Sisters, Evangelist Fred, Pastor Cyril, Mike Tamakloe, Prince Duah. We say thank you for your faith in Christ and the for the work you do for Him.

23. For the wonderful Pastors and their wives that we are working with in the Ghana Assemblies of God Fellowship in Canada we say God bless you: Rev. Milton and Mrs. Priscila Offei, Rev. Isaac and Mrs. Tina Bonful, Rev. Anthony and Rev. Mrs. Rose Nyanzu, Rev. Jonathan and Mrs. Doreen Manu, Rev. Boniface and Mrs. Evelyn Keelson, Rev. Douglas and Mrs. Elizabeth Owusu Ansah.

24. For the wonderful and amazing staff at Living Word Assembly of God; Mrs. Victoria Marfo, Pastor Cheryl, and Pastor Cyril and Mrs. Freda Opoku. God bless you for labouring with us for souls.

25. For the families of Amoah-Awuah and Rev. Madjitey who trusted us with their children who are studying in Canada, may the Lord grant you more grace. To David and Joana, we say thank you.

Who can you thank God for in your life? Why do you have to be grateful to God and the people in your life?

Always remember that:

"Gratitude is the healthiest of all human emotions. The more you express gratitude for what you have, the more likely you will have even more to express gratitude for"— **Zig Ziglar**

8

25 LESSONS IN 25 MARRIAGE YEARS

"This journey called life is never short of teachable moments and life lessons. We live. We learn. Rinse. Repeat. Life experiences are like little breadcrumbs of wisdom, equipping us for the next curveball or unexpected turn" **—Unknown**

The journey which began with us from the Campus of the University of Ghana Legon in the early 90's brought us together as Christian brother and sister, moved into two lovers and after 25 years we still love and cherish each other for the life and love we have shared graciously together after responding "I do" to each other in the presence of God, our friends, families and the officiating minister Rev. Ofosuhene, and our premarital, marriage councillor, late Rev. Yeboah-Duah, on May 6, 1995, at the Police Church Cathedral near the 37 Military Hospital in Accra. The journey has taught us many lessons of which we present 25 of them for your reflection:

1. Each of you be a lover of one person-Christ
2. Pray to hear and love God as individuals
3. Pray together daily even if it's for just 25 minutes
4. Study the Word together at least once a week
5. Give all the money to the woman and support her manage it
6. Fast and pray together as a couple
7. Say I am sorry and mean it
8. Say I am thankful and mean it
9. Say I Love you and mean it
10. Say I forgive you and mean it
11. Say the food taste good and mean it
12. Say you are beautiful and mean it
13. Say your dress is great on you and mean it
14. Say your hair is well styled and mean it
15. Be content with what you have and mean it
16. Say you will Live within your means and mean it
17. Say you are called into the ministry and mean it
18. Say you admit your mistake and mean it
19. Say you will support with house chores and mean it
20. Honour, praise, respect each other both privately and publicly and mean it.
21. Remember birthdays, anniversaries, special events and celebrate it meaningfully

22. Say you will go on a retreat and mean it
23. Say you will go on vacation and mean it
24. Say you will pray for each other and mean it
25. Stay spirit led, Word directed, ministry focused, heaven inspired and spouse admirer and mean it.

Always remember that:

"You only struggle because you're ready to grow but aren't willing to let go." — ***Drew Gerald***

9

25 MARRIAGE QUESTIONS TO REVIEW

"Judge a man by his questions rather than by his answers." — **Voltaire**

We thought of the power of questions and the benefits of questions in the life of the married, so provided these for reflection and contemplation as you journey through your married life. We believe that right answers will lead you to the right solutions that will ultimately result into the right kind of marriage for you.

1. Are you in love?
2. How do you know?
3. What is love to you?
4. How are husbands supposed to love their wives?
5. How do you love somebody you say you love?
6. What is romance to you?
7. Are you romantic?

8. How do you tell?
9. Are you selfless?
10. What is selflessness?
11. How do you continue to be selfless?
12. What is respect?
13. Do you respect your spouse?
14. How do you increase your respect temperature?
15. How do you increase your love temperature in your marriage?
16. What do you understand by the word submit?
17. How do you know you are submissive?
18. How do you measure your submission temperature?
19. What is an idol?
20. How do you know your marriage, kids, money, work, ministry and pleasure has not become an idol to you?
21. How do you measure your love for God, love for His Word and love for His world?
22. What is freshness? How do you ensure your freshness in your marriage?
23. What is intimacy? How do you intentionally stay intimate?
24. What is legacy?
25. What marriage legacy do you want to leave after you are dead and gone? How do you want to be remembered by your family?

Note in questioning, that:

"Most misunderstandings in the world could be avoided if people would simply take the time to ask, "What else could this mean?"— Shannon L. Alder

10

25 NUGGETS FROM THE 25 PLUS

Studying goes deeper than mere reading. There are surface nuggets to be gathered but the best of the gold is underneath, and it takes time and labor to secure it—**Mary McLeod Bethune**

In a recent study conducted by the Journal of Social Psychological and Personality Science (SPPS), researchers discovered people with religious affiliations (communities) lived between 5.64 and 9.45 years longer than those with no religious affiliation. The American Council on Science and Health further correlated volunteer and social opportunities offered within religious communities' attribute to longer life spans, stating the true health benefits lie within the social interaction and relationships formed within a like-minded community.

Ye shall walk in all the ways which the LORD your God hath commanded you, that ye may live, and that it may be well with you, and that ye may prolong your days in the land which ye shall possess. Deuteronomy 5:33

This part seeks to bring lessons from our seniors in marriage. Marriage as God has ordained and established is doable. If you are wondering whether you can make it or not let these practical and real-life examples help you and be of a blessing to you. Learn, live, listen, love, lead and marry till we meet in heaven and never regret having met each other on earth.

1. *John and Wendy (Gwendolyn) Pullen*

John and Wendy (Gwendolyn) Pullen are celebrating 50 years of marriage—March 7, 1970—Monson, Maine. They have this to say about the secret of their successful marriage: "Patience, flexibility and commitment on the front end that I'm choosing for the rest of my life to be committed to this man or woman till death do us part—the decision aside the fantasies."

2. Dr. Philip and Marcia Eyster

They say: "To have a successful marriage for 39 years you just must make the decision to marry a smart woman and you will be safe, secured and celebrated."

3. President Jimmy Carter and Rosalynn Carter

The former President Jimmy Carter and his wife, Rosalynn Carter, celebrated their 73rd wedding anniversary, making them the longest married presidential couple in history. Many factors go into marital longevity, including a person's age at marriage, faith in the Lord, wealth, education level, and geographic location, But the secret to the Carters' success might be as simple as the fact that, well, they **chose** to stay together (according to CNN reporter).

4. Rev. Dr. John and Mrs. Vivacious Veronica Ghartey

Rev. Dr. John and Mrs. Vivacious Veronica Ghartey, after 36 years of marriage believe that marriage has a four-fold purpose. It is a call to partnership or mutual help and comfort, to procreation of children, to pleasure and to purity, both in acts and thoughts.

Marriage's essential features are forgiveness, forgetfulness, forbearance, flexibility, friendship, fun, faithfulness, freedom, frankness, fulfillment, fairness, fondness, and fellowship.

5. *Pastor John and Mrs. Lee Willis*

Pastor John and Mrs. Lee Willis after 40 years of marriages affirm that the secret to their marriage is to marry a wife and husband who loves God; yes one who just loves God.

6. *Mr. Steve and Mrs. Tracy Gibbs*

Mr. Steve and Mrs. Tracy Gibbs after years of marriage reveal their secret thus: "A wise fellow (my older brother) once told me: 'marriage is not a 50-50 arrangement. Both husband and wife have to be willing to give 100% of themselves to the other. If each is willing to do that, the chances for a successful marriage are very good'. He was right."

7. *Rev. Joseph and Mrs. Mary Osei-Amoah*

Rev. Joseph and Mrs. Mary Osei-Amoah after being married for 51 years, assert and affirm that marriage is instituted by God and so one should marry with the manual of God in heart and mind—

the Bible. On the question of their advice for the newly wed, they had the following nuggets to give:

> Learn to live in love and create a peaceful and a happy home. Developing a happy home calls for adjustments for both husband and wife. Acknowledge that marriage is a lifetime job and so ask God for His help, ask for wisdom, insight and divine guidance.
>
> We believe that healthy-lasting marriages take prayer and patience. Make the decision that we are both coming into the marriage with our baggage from our upbringing and so must be aware and willing to work on our weaknesses. We focus on the good things in each other and emphasize that instead of the weaknesses. Pray for yourself first and for your partner. Forgive each other and be open with each other about what you might be going through. When you are resolving your issues or addressing any misunderstanding listen patiently and wait for the right time to talk through it. Listen to understand not to be understood.
>
> We have learnt to avoid external influences in our marriage particularly from parents and friends.
>
> When it comes to money, spend within your means. Do not buy things with the money you do not have.

Proverbs 31 reveals the roles and responsibilities for both husband and wife. What needs to happen is to appreciate and help each other to handle the chores at home. And finally, do not deprive yourselves when it comes to sex. Handle it with wisdom, time, tact and understanding.

The key is to agree to attend the same church as a married couple right from the onset.

Pay attention to these scriptures for your good:

"A gentle answer turns away wrath, but a harsh word stirs up anger."—Proverbs 15:1

"My dear brothers and sisters, take note of this: Everyone should be quick to listen, slow to speak and slow to become angry, because human anger does not produce the righteousness that God desires."—James 1:19-20.

8. Jewish liberator of Nazi camp, wife of 78 years dies hours apart.

LONGMEADOW, Massachusetts — A World War II veteran and his wife of nearly eight decades who had tested positive for COVID-19 died together on the same day. David and Muriel Cohen died within hours of each other at a Longmeadow nursing home on April 10. Muriel, 97, had tested positive for the virus and

David, 102, had been sick but his test results came back negative. The couple decided to remain together even as the Jewish Nursing Home tried to transfer residents who were infected to a separate unit. Fran Grosnick, their daughter, gave the nursing home permission to let her parents stay together. They have always been together holding hands. What a testimony, one of the key to healthy long-lasting marriage is holding hands, not sometimes but always.

9. Mr. Kofi and Irene Amoa-Awuah

Mr. Kofi Amoa-Awuah and wife, Irene Amoa-Awuah, who have been married since 1993, that is after 27 years and counting, had the following to say:

> Communication between couples is key, keeping the channels open at all times, and dealing with misunderstandings as and when they crop up. Mutual respect for each other at all times.

According to them, each party to the marriage should be reasonably matured in emotions and Christian life and should have reasonable economic resources and they should give reasonable expectations of each other.

10. Rev. Eric and Mrs. Felicia Amoah

Rev. Eric Amoah and Mrs. Felicia Amoah after 37 years of marriage and counting have these truths regarding healthy, longer and godly marriages:

Patience and tolerance have been the secret that has held us together.

Patience, in that all good things take time to mature… expectations coming into marriage will take time to mature and hence requires patience.

We have had our share of pulls and tugs in the earlier days, but we waited on the Lord to mature us. Patience has been our guiding principle even when we do not agree.

Expect to give in marriage as opposed to getting. You will always get back more than you give. Unrealistic expectation was one of our greatest challenges in our earlier years that almost derailed the marriage. Proper counselling before marriage would have helped a lot in this area had we have one.

Tolerance in marriage is to understand that each is coming from different upbringing, and family backgrounds. This is where I have seen so many marriages fall apart when this basic awareness is not noted and addressed earlier in the marriage. Approach to things, manner of speaking and attitudes will differ. Tolerance is needed as you begin to learn from each other, forge a new identity together, something that both of you can call your own. It may be gleaned from each others background, but they will be your own.

Tolerance is always needed when people of different backgrounds but with one common goal come together. The Apostle Paul encouraged the believers in the church of Ephesus, "*2 Be completely humble and gentle; be patient, bearing with one another in love. 3 Make every effort to keep the unity of the Spirit through the bond of peace. 4 There is one body and one Spirit, just as you were called to one hope when you were called; 5 one Lord, one faith, one baptism; 6 one God and Father of all, who is over all and through all and in all.*" Eph. 4:2-6.

Trust, like Love, is the glue that has kept us going. It has allowed sound financial planning and less stress that could result in frustrations and tensions related illness.

11. *Rev. Dr. David and Mrs. Susan Wells*

Rev. Dr. David and Mrs. Susan Wells' posting on Facebook on their 45th anniversary had this to share with the world of the secret to their healthy, strong, and long-lasting marriage:

As I celebrate with Susan McQuinn Wells our 45th Anniversary and continue to observe and enjoy her loving care, her spunk and her zest for a life lived with purpose, I was reminded of the following observation I noted in a recent article regarding our shared life and calling together.

The most influential peer in the development of my character and spirit walked into my life during our first year in college. Susan Patricia Ann Marie McQuinn, a spunky French-Irish-Loyalist woman from Campbellton, N.B., appeared in our class a week late with everything she owned in a shipping trunk. She was lively, intelligent, funny, attractive, and had a clear leadership calling from the Lord. She was passionate for Him and for people to come to know Jesus.

My world was rocked, so I did what every young man turning 18 does when he wants to attract a young woman. I made fun of her—in this case, of her New Brunswick North Shore accent. That went over really well!

Summed up in one paragraph, here's the thing. A young man from Alberta who was called by God and wanted to follow Jesus completely entered a loving marriage covenant with a young woman from New Brunswick who was called by God and wanted to follow Jesus completely. This mutuality of calling to God and to each other has been absolutely the greatest influence in each of our lives for becoming more like Jesus, and for fulfilling His purpose for our lives. For many of us as young adults, the person we choose as the number one human influence in our lives often determines if Jesus can shape us into all we are called to be." So very grateful to God for Susan's loving influence in my life.

12. *Sammy and Macie Waller*

75 Years and having been married for 50 years, when asked the following questions, Sammy and Macie had this to say:

WHAT'S THE SECRET TO YOUR MARRIAGE?

Macie: "I don't really know if there're any secrets. We just respect each other, and we love each other. We're best friends."
Sammy: "We don't do a lot of arguing. We try to get along most of the time and we get along pretty good. We do things together. We go to the movies—we don't like the movies anymore—but we just got along. I didn't go to the bar and leave her home and she didn't go to places and leave me home. We just hung together. I'm still hanging.

HOW DO YOU RESOLVE CONFLICT THE BEST?

Macie: "We just talk it over and try to straighten it out."

Sammy: "I just normally shut up. I don't say a word."

13. Frank and Thelma Hoffman

67 Years and married for 50 years, revealed the following in answer to the following questions:

WHAT'S THE SECRET TO YOUR MARRIAGE?

Thelma: "Loving one another and a lot of patience and knowing what's important in life."

Frank: "Love and a wonderful companionship. That is the great secret. We like to do most of the same things ... like go on cruises, go to the movies, go to concerts and socialize with friends."

HOW DO YOU RESOLVE CONFLICT THE BEST?

Thelma: "He doesn't argue. He doesn't fight. It's very difficult to make a point when you're doing the arguing; he just will not argue."

Frank: "Easy! She wins! ... But we work it out and we get along. We go forward. We're both understanding and can appreciate each point of view, and we try to correct those problems. It's discussed and dropped."

14. *James and Virginia Wilson*

63 Years of marriage, when asked the following questions about marriage, responded with these life-transforming answers:

WHAT IS THE SECRET TO YOUR MARRIAGE?

Virginia: Communication. We try to communicate with each other. In our earlier years, he was a band director—for 40 years—which means that he was busy, busy, busy. And I was an elementary school teacher… so we had to communicate often."

James: "Well, we love each other. And we come from parents who were church-going folks, and they taught us [about marriage] and we respected them, so we had no problems. We lived the example they put forth for us."

HOW DO YOU RESOLVE CONFLICT THE BEST?

Virginia: "Talk it over. If you don't get it done today, talk about it in the morning, talk about it in the afternoon."

James: "We have so few conflicts, but we talk about it. She expresses her side and I express mine."

15. Stewart and Sandra Brown

My name is Stewart Brown and I have been married to an amazing woman named Sandra. In our 41 years of marriage, we have learned some "secrets" of a healthy and lasting marriage:

Always begin with God! When I was feeling lonely and looking for a young woman whom I could marry, it soon became obvious that I could not find that one "right" girl for me. In dating various girls, I eventually learned that first impressions were not necessarily proof that this was the one. Like most young men, I looked first at the "outward appearance. In His grace, God saved me from this unwise way in making correct decisions. So, wise words such as Psalm 32:8-9 became important tools for me in finding the right life mate. God knew the heart of a young woman named Sandra and how we could complement each other and experience fulfillment within God's plan. Once I trusted the Lord to direct me, my path to His choice for me became much clearer!

View your prospective life mate from God's perspective, from a spiritual viewpoint. A person may look very attractive or handsome in the body but be the opposite in their attitude, character, and spiritual demeanor.

Ask other godly or Christ-like family and friends to share their observations of the two of you together. Do they sense that you both love the Lord and that you are willing to be partners and not competitors?

Once you do marry, determine that you and your spouse will make God your priority. If you grow in your love for the Lord Jesus, you will then grow in your love for each other. Sandra and I have truly experienced the joy of Christ as we determine not to use the other for selfish purposes, but we choose to serve each other for the glory of God. As Philippians 2:3 teaches, we treat the other as more important than ourselves. So, I want to serve God, then to serve Sandra in any and every situation so that she can become all that God desires her to be. So, as Ephesians 5:21-33 tells us, healthy marriage is always based on the practise of Christ-like sacrificial love and respect, never based on mere feelings!

Our decision to marry was never included the option of divorce. Both Sandra and I knew that marriage was permanent— "until death do us part". We chose to love each other—a total commitment regardless of the circumstances. If you go into a marriage thinking that you can opt out if you don't like it, your marriage would be a failure from the beginning. Know God's will. If you allow Him to lead you, you will grow and blossom to the end!

We know that the best environment to raise children to know the Lord is for them to see how we, as their parents, love each other even when or if we disagree on anything.

Sandra and I now see our marriage as a permanent exclusive covenant relationship reflecting the community of God the Father, Son, and Holy Spirit and not a convenient arrangement just to supply our wants!

16. Lewis and Marsha McGehee

Lewis and Marsha McGehee, married for 44 years, assert:

> Reminisce about why you first fell in love. Your passion for one another may wax and wane over the years but remembering why you first fell in love can help pull you back in when you feel like you're drifting away from each other. "Keep close in your mind some poignant memories of the first rushes of love—when you knew that you never wanted to be far from this person, when your heart felt a physical jump at the sight of them," say Lewis and Marsha McGehee, who have been married for 44 years. "The daily

obstacles will work out if the resolve to hold on to your love story is strong."

Looking for excuses to end things, throwing out the "D" word in arguments—or even thinking that this fight might be your last one—will inevitably cause tension in your marriage that you may be unable to fix.

"Never go into an argument thinking that it could be the end of the relationship," the McGehees advise. "That means speaking your mind, but not saying or doing anything that is not recoverable. Healthy marriages are not always smooth but should always be respectful."

17. Carol Gee

Celebrate: Celebrate one another just because! You shouldn't wait for holidays or anniversaries to celebrate all the wonderful things you love about your spouse. "I have always celebrated birthdays, anniversaries, and it simply being a Wednesday on what started as a crazy work week," says Carol Gee, author of *Random Notes (About Life, "Stuff" And Finally Learning To Exhale)*, who has been married for 47 years. "Celebrate occasions, big and small. These celebrations don't have to be big deals—a cake and coffee to celebrate a birthday, or because it's Friday and you simply love being together." "One day I asked my husband what he thought the secret to our marriage was," says Gee. "A quiet man of little words, he said, 'I never know what you are going to do from one minute to the next, and I find I like that.'"

18. Rev. Dr. Augustine Adu-Anane and Rev. Mrs. Eleanor Adu-Anane

Rev. Dr. Augustine Adu-Anane and Rev Mrs. Eleanor Adu-Anane who have been married since 1987, that is about 33 years, reveal that the secret to their healthy, long-lasting marriage is based on these few practices:

> Everyone in marriage or going into marriage should understand the concept of how to complete and complement each other. This means that no one is perfect and therefore, will need each other. Each person should be prepared to complement and celebrate each other's strengths and work towards improving our weaknesses.
>
> This requires:
> 1. Commitment: Commit yourself wholeheartedly to help your partner grow and turn the weaknesses to strengths
> 2. Acceptance: Accept each other regardless of their different background and upbringing, lifestyles, and

attitudes, knowing that there is room for improvement.

3. Openness: Openness brings trust so be open to each other especially in communication and finance
4. Trustworthiness: Try as much as possible not to give your partner any cause to doubt you
5. Finally, be sexy and ready for sex all the time and help do house chores together

These have been so helpful for our 33 years journey in marriage which is still going strong.

19. Deacon Felix and Mrs. Charity Oppong-Kyekyeku

Deacon Felix Oppong-Kyekyeku and Mrs. Charity Oppong-Kyekyeku, who have been married for about 29 years and counting, had the A.D.A.P.T nugget to share:

> Marriage is a union between two imperfect people. Therefore, for a couple to experience health, success, enjoyment, and longevity in their marriage, the two must be willing to adapt to each other in a loving manner.
>
> My advice to newly-weds and prospective couples is summarized with the acronym for the word ADAPT

which I have created and constantly apply in my 29 years of a blessed marriage with Charity.

A—Admit

Remember you are not a perfect wife or husband; therefore, you are prone to make mistakes or even commit offences. Therefore, be quick to admit your wrongs, apologize and move on. Do not give the devil a foothold to become a stronghold in your marriage.

D—Devotion

Be devoted to each other. I have often said to my co-workers that my wife is the most beautiful and loving woman in the world, therefore I will not give my attention to any other woman. Such a mindset fuels loyalty and faithfulness to each other in marriage.

A—Accountability

A person who is not accountable to anybody will lead an undisciplined life. As imperfect people, we all need others to "check us" so that we do not go astray. Always remember that you do not own yourself as a husband or wife, you are two people joined together as one flesh. Therefore, be accountable to each other in perfect unity.

P—Prayer

Someone has said that " The family that prays together stays together"

I am always strengthened and encouraged when I pray with my wife alone. There is something about a husband and wife kneeling side by side each other and crying to the Lord together. There is healing from any resentments and bitterness towards each other, refreshment from the Holy Spirit and an experience of the presence of God. Do not underestimate the power of prayer in your marriage. Pray for your wife or husband every day.

T—Trust

Trust is an indispensable virtue that a couple must cultivate in order to build and maintain a healthy, successful and a happy marriage. Where there is trust for each other there will be no suspicion of unfaithfulness in a marriage and misuse of family resources. We must develop trust for each other by being honest with regards to finances, friends, and families. A breakdown of trust will result in an unhealthy relationship. Can your spouse trust you with his/her bank or credit card and passwords? Be a trustworthy husband or wife and enjoy a long-lasting marriage.

While these ingredients are by no means exhaustive, they have been the foundation and the building blocks of my marriage with my lovely wife Charity for the past twenty-nine years. Try them and you will experience a joyful, healthy, and a successful marriage as long as "You Both Shall Live".

20. Dr. Jacob and Mrs. Ivy Stella Otchere Al Hassan

Dr. Jacob Al Hassan and Mrs. Ivy Stella Otchere-Al Hassan celebrating their 29 years of blessed marriage in their answer to the question, "What will you offer newly-weds or will-be couples about the secret of the success, health, and longevity of your marriage?", convincingly said this:

> We have always considered our marriage as a lasting covenant between GOD and ourselves. Therefore, Paul's admonition to "husbands to love their wife as Christ loved the church..." (Eph 5:25) and "wives to submit to their husbands..." (Eph 5:22) has always propelled us over the years to overcome all the challenges that occur in intertribal marriages like ours. These verses have enabled us to embrace Christ's finished work on Calvary for the church as a yardstick for the sacrificial and unconditional love in our marriage"

21. Mr. and Mrs. Emmanuel and Comfort Ayiku

Mr. and Mrs. Emmanuel and Comfort Ayiku precious saints who have been married for about 31 years give the following nuggets:

> Marriage to us is a gift from God and for that reason, we always try our best through prayer to maintain it in good shape so that when God, the Giver, looks at us in our marriage, He will feel proud of us.
>
> In simplest term, marriage to us is more than a physical union between us but also as part of our service to God to honor Him with joy and gladness.
>
> Our advice to the younger generation is that marriage is honorable so they should make every effort through prayer and the reading of the Word of God to maintain it as such.
>
> God instituted marriage for companionship and enjoyment as part of our daily normal living and building families so they should pray to God for grace to help them fulfil the God-given mandate for mankind.
>
> From these life examples, our desire is to seek to reveal that there are indeed many marriages that have and are still standing the test of time to build healthy, godly, long lasting, and happy marriages in our world. Do not be deceived by the divorce rates but be encouraged and

motivated by the many examples of healthy marriages around you.

22. Rev. Isaac and Mrs. Tina Bonful

Married for over 30 years, when asked, "What will you offer newly-weds or will-be couples about the secret of the success, health, and longevity of your marriage?", Rev. Isaac and Tina had this to say:

> The first thing we would say is that marriage is God's idea and so we need to have God's mind regarding it. It should not be our culture's way of looking at marriage but God's way. God's way is found in His Word so couples must study the Bible and pray together. Couples must also pray for each other.
>
> The next thing is that couples must respect each other, and this means we must be courteous to each other. Under no circumstances should couples hurl insults at one another. This respect must be extended to each other's family and so there should be no running down of each other's family member.
>
> It is important not to take one another for granted. As couples settle down in marriage, the tendency is to take each other for granted. It must be noted that marriage is a

lifelong journey and not an event. What couples do to each other after marriage goes a long way to make or break the union. Even though life can be serious, there should always be time to play and laugh with each other.

The role of sex in the marriage must not be downplayed. Sex is a bonding agent and so couples should not toy with this aspect of their life. It cements the relationship. Do not allow unforgiveness to destroy this all-important area of your relationship.

Each partner in the marriage must decide that he/she would do everything necessary to make the marriage thrive.

Practise transparency in the marriage. Do not hide things from each other. Discuss your finances and everything that ought to be discussed. Trust is key in every marriage. Use positive language in your discussions.

23. *Deacon Larry Kutuadu and Mrs. Comfort Kutuadu*

Deacon Larry Kutuadu and Mrs. Comfort Kutuadu, have been married for about 44 years by the grace of God. They had the following to say when asked, "What will you offer newly-weds or will-be couples about the secret of the success, health, and longevity of your marriage?":

> I have learnt that when people look for a secret for the success of another in some area of life, there is usually no secret at all. The truth is that we are all different and will be exposed to different and changing circumstances. Given that, I submit that we should build our lives and values on what is unchanging. Ten years into our marriage, after I got saved, I learnt, understood, and resolved that my marriage is first a commitment to God, then to my wife. Just as I trust God to help me walk in faith, my marriage is an essential part of this faith life, and it honours God when we succeed. All other values of love, affection, respect, and the practices of duty, responsibility, conflict resolution, and the like, flow from this commitment to God. This foundation helped me to always remember that failure is not an option. I guess it has worked. There have been mistakes, downtimes, challenges, and disappointments but the blessings, pleasures, joys, rewards, and lasting memories of love and companionship outweigh the former. Marriage is good; go ahead and make yours great.

24. Rev Christian and Mrs. Vivian Essandoh

My good and great friend and brother Rev. Essandoh, who has been married for 27 years, when asked about the secret of a successful marriage, penned down their story:

Hello Bishop (my nick name),

Until you asked me to send you my story of a successful marriage, I had not taken the trouble to think about the matter. Honestly, your request has forced me to cast a retrospective glance at my marriage journey; and I have asked myself, "how come for twenty-seven years of marriage we have had little life-threatening challenges to our marriage, apart from the little, little skirmishes that are common to every marriage." Your request has again challenged me to ask, "what does it mean to have a successful marriage?"

Is a successful marriage one without the existential challenges that confronts marriages? Is it to marry and progress in life, realizing your dreams and aspirations? Is it to continue until one of the two is no more?

I do not know what definition you are giving to a "successful marriage." But however, you define it, I think from the Bible's point of view, a successful marriage is one in which the two have become one flesh. It is as simple as that. Any marriage that does not travel to that point cannot be said to be successful. Many leave and cleave, but most do not attain the one flesh status. It is at the one flesh stage that one can claim to have a successful marriage.

I have seen couples go as far as twenty, thirty, fifty years in marriage and still divorce. So, longevity in marriage is not a sign of a successful marriage. A couple can live their separate lives in their relationship and not worry themselves, as long as each one is comfortable with what he or she is doing, the marriage will continue. But that cannot be a successful marriage.

I believe a successful marriage can be describe as that relationship where one considers that he or she belongs to the other person and is there for the interest of the other person.

As you may be aware, if my concern is my wife's concern, and if her interest is my interest, and we can serve each other without complaining, and if we can share what we acquire individually with each other, as belonging to all of us, that marriage is successful. And that is my story.

For twenty-seven years, Vivian and I have been there for each other and building our family without a feel of regret, disappointment, or a potential threat for divorce. I cannot be proud, it is not as if we do not go through the challenges every marriage goes through, (we are still human) but those challenges have rather built us up than destroy us. Raising the children, and the children themselves, have not been able to threaten our relationship. Our in-laws, finances and sex have not been able to divide us either. In our part of the world, it is believed that this trio – in-laws, finances, and sex – are the three demons that threatens the success of every marriage. Reflecting over our journey, I see one virtue that has helped us come this far. It is the attitude of selflessness.

Seriously, I believe without this attitude Vivian and I could not continue to this point. Both of us are coming from poor backgrounds. Simply that. Viv is the key person in her family who supports the family, just like me. We have helped her siblings go through school and are still helping some of her family members. Likewise, I cater for almost all my siblings and have helped my siblings go through school and learn vocation. We are still taking care of our family members while seeing our own children through school. That is a huge responsibility and a toll on our meager resources. But how could we do this, except that we feel we are there for each other, and are ready to support ourselves with cheerful readiness. If it were not for selflessness, at least one of us might have been tired. That is one unique characteristics of selflessness. You do not get tired giving to the other person.

Reflecting over the attitude of selflessness, I have observed that the selfless person does not usually count the cost but rather the care that can be given. Again, it seems to me that the selfless person is usually unconscious of his or her virtue, and therefore does not expect any reward in return for his or her self-giving.

During pre-marital counseling, we are given different methods of financial management, which we can adopt to help us take control of our finances. Vivian and I have a different approach. She keeps her account and I keep my account. She knows how much comes in and I know how much she owes. She sometimes conducts my banking transactions, apart from signing a cheque. We have that freedom of managing our personal accounts but have never, I repeat with all sincerity, have never had financial scuffles in our marriage before. Not what I can remember. The secret is selflessness. I do not think I have anything to hide about my finances, neither does she. This is the beauty of selflessness, it does not withhold unnecessarily, but freely gives to support the other person. A selfish person will not only withhold, but hide, conceal, and give an impression he has nothing. This brings to mind a day Vivian gave me a surprise by handing over to me the document of a landed property she bought in our name – two plots of land.

Again, with selflessness, responsibilities, and duties merge into a dedicated service for the upliftment of the other person; you give up yourself to serve the other without complaining or arguing.

When I clean my room or lay the bed, or take care of chores at home, it does not appear I am obligated to do so. I usually do the chores because I feel she should not do everything. You know, most of the times the children are in school, and we are left alone in the house.

The least I can say about our sex life the better. *Asempa ye tia.* (a good story is said in few words)—but it is because of selflessness.

You know what? It is twenty-seven years now, since we got married, but up till today, when I am gone for over a week, by the time I return one or two of my suits will be hanging in the bedroom, out of the wardrobe. When you ask, she will tell you, "I was missing you, and brought them out to feel you around." I do not do that, but I always wished I were back home, whenever I travelled away from home for a week or two. It does not matter where I had been on the globe, I always missed home and wished I could go back, if not for what I may be doing. I think this is what I call a successful marriage. It is the two enjoying each other as companions; it is the two sharing their lives together and not feeling being cheated; it is the two supporting each other through his or her challenges; it is the two building a home where they feel belonging. Such is a successful marriage.

25. Rev. Professor Paul and Rev Mrs. Gladys Frimpong-Manso

Rev. Professor and Rev. Mrs. Gladys Frimpong-Manso who were joined in holy matrimony on April 8, 1984, that is about 36 years ago, had these to admonish will-be couples with:

> We went into the marriage acknowledging that we cannot make it without the fear of God, we knew what it meant to be married. We made the decision on the frontend to go into the marriage relationship with a never turning back attitude. We believed and lived by the mantra that it was meant for better for worse or for richer or for poorer.
>
> Some of the attitudes and conducts that has kept us together all these while and believe will continue to do are but not limited to:
>
> ♥ Mutual respect and trust for one another. We honor each other genuinely and never take each other for granted.

- ♥ Cultivating a lively communication with transparency in all things and in every areas of your lives. We do not bear grudge against each other but ask for forgiveness of each other as quick as possible and forgive ourselves without resentments.

- ♥ The Scriptures and Christ plays a central role in our home as a result we dedicate ourselves to have our Family devotions daily. We schedule time, mostly in the evenings to study the Bible and pray together.

- ♥ We are very much interested in God and the things of God. We prioritize God and so ensure our diligence in honoring God with our tithe, and offerings. We go the extra mile to support God's work with all our being. The truth is God has never ever failed to seek our interest too.

- ♥ We Play and joke a lot with each other but not laugh at each other. This attitude, we have observed, has helped us to overcome anger and temper.

- ♥ As a husband I seek to understand my wife very well and handle her as the weaker vessel who is so special and important to me.

- ♥ We do not live our lives as individuals who seem to be on, what I will call "fault-finding expedition"

- ♥ We believe and affirm that the longer couples stay together, the better and the more matured, healthy and stronger they should be as a couple. We are far, far better than we were ten years or twenty years ago and we are very grateful to God.

- ♥ We ensure that we have Respect for each others' families and not just ours.

Olivia and I trust that these real-life examples have been an encouragement to you. We will love for you to also send us your story for future use when we turn fifty years in marriage and putting together our future book "*50 Nuggets at 50*". May the Lord bless you and grant you the grace to build a long, lasting and healthy marriage in Jesus name! Shout a big …Amen!

11

25 MARRIAGE JOKES FOR LAUGHS

"A day without laughter is a day wasted."—Charlie Chaplin

There are many clean jokes out there, including ones based on the Bible, Christianity, and Jesus. We hope these jokes will help you do what we did when we were writing and working on the book-LAUGH with tears. Laughing is an amazing gift from God. It helps you cope with sadness and everyday life. Have you ever felt mad and then someone said something to make you laugh? Even though you were upset the laughter made your heart feel better. Laughter is medicine to the bones. Read, laugh, learn and be healed!

1. A woman is unpredictable. Before marriage, she *expects* a man, after marriage she *suspects* him, and after death she *respects* him.

2. There was this guy who told his woman that he loved her so much that he would go through hell for her. They got married—and now he is going through hell.

3. A man inserted an advertisement online and through social media: "*Wife Wanted*" The next day, his inbox was inundated with hundreds of emails, texts, and WhatsApp messages. They all said the same thing, "you can have mine".

4. When a man opens the door of his car for his wife, you can be sure of one thing: either the car is new, or the wife is new.

5. A man received a note from some kidnappers. The note stated: "If you don't promise to send us $100,000, we promise you we will kidnap your wife". The poor man wrote back, "I am afraid I can't keep my promise, but I hope you will keep yours".

6. A woman lost her husband through a tragic accident and was mourning him at a funeral. However, she noticed that her friend was weeping and wailing even more than she herself did. It was so serious that she became suspicious that her friend might have had something to do with her late husband. She mustered courage and inquired from her friend why that somber grief. The friend, without hesitation, replied, "God is

not fair; He took away a good man, and left the monster in my home. How I wish He would have taken mine instead".

7. If you ask her to do something, she does not enjoy, that's domination. If she asks you, it is a favor.
If you buy her flowers, you are after something. If you do not, you are not thoughtful.
If you cry, you are a wimp. If you do not, you are insensitive.
If you get a promotion ahead of her, it is favoritism. If she gets a job ahead of you, it is equal opportunity.

8. Attending a wedding for the first time, a little girl whispered to her mother, "Why is the bride dressed in white?" "Because white is the color of happiness, and today is the happiest day of her life." The child thought about this for a moment, then said, "So why is the groom wearing black?"

9. In heaven there were two lines. One said, "Men who were bossed by their wives," and the other one said, "Men who weren't bossed by their wives". There was a big line for the first one, but then the man who was checking people's name in the Book of Life saw one man in the other line. So, he told the guys to wait. He asked the man why he was in that line. The man replied, "My wife told me to."

10. A woman decided to have her portrait painted. She told the artist, "Paint me with diamond rings, a diamond necklace, emerald bracelets, a ruby broach, and gold Rolex." "But you are not wearing any of those things," he replied. "I know," she said. "It's in case I should die before my husband. I'm sure he will remarry right away, and I want his new wife to go crazy looking for the jewellery."

11. The child was a typical four-year-old girl - cute, inquisitive, bright as a new penny. When she expressed difficulty in grasping the concept of marriage, her father decided to pull out his wedding photo album, thinking visual images would help. One page after another, he pointed out the bride arriving at the church, the entrance, the wedding ceremony, the recessional, the reception, etc. "Now do you understand?" he asked. "I think so," she said, "is that when mommy came to work for us?"

12. A woman awoke during the night to find that her husband was not in bed. She put on her robe and went downstairs. He was sitting at the kitchen table with a cup of coffee in front of him. He appeared to be in deep thought, just staring at the wall. She saw him wipe a tear from his eye and take a sip of his coffee. "What's the matter dear? Why are you down here at this time of night?" she asked. "Do you remember twenty years ago

when we were dating, and you were only 16?" he asked. "Yes, I do," she replied. "Do you remember when your father caught us in the back seat of my car kissing?" "Yes, I remember." "Do you remember when he shoved that shotgun in my face and said, 'Either you marry my daughter or spend twenty years in jail?'" "Yes, I do," she said. He wiped another tear from his cheek and said, "You know...I would have gotten out today."

13. A couple drove several miles down a country road, not saying a word. An earlier discussion had led to an argument, and neither wanted to concede their position. As they passed a barnyard of mules and pigs, the husband sarcastically asked, "Relatives of yours?" "Yep," the wife replied, "In-laws."

14. As soon as the newlyweds returned from their honeymoon, the young bride called her mother, who lived a couple of hours away. "How did everything go?" her mom asked. "Oh, mother," she began, "The honeymoon was wonderful! So romantic, we had a terrific time. But, mother, on our way back, Andy started using really horrible language. Stuff I had never heard before. Really terrible four-letter words. You have got to come get me and take me home. Please, Mother!" the new bride sobbed over the telephone. "But, honey," the mother countered, "What four-letter words?" "I can't tell you, mother,

they're too awful! Come get me, please!" "Darling, you must tell me what has gotten you so upset.... Tell mother what four-letter words he used." Still sobbing, the bride said, "Mother, words like dust, wash, iron, cook."

15. During the wedding rehearsal, the groom approached the minister with an unusual offer. "Look, I'll give you $100 if you'll change the wedding vows. When you get to me and the part where I'm to promise to 'love, honor and obey' and 'forsaking all others, be faithful to her forever,' I'd appreciate it if you'd just leave that part out." He passed the minister the cash and walked away satisfied. The wedding day arrives, and the bride and groom have moved to that part of the ceremony where the vows are exchanged. When it comes time for the groom's vows, the minister looks the young man in the eye and says, "Will you promise to prostrate yourself before her, obey her every command and wish, serve her breakfast in bed every morning of your life and swear eternally before God and your lovely wife that you will not ever even look at another woman, as long as you both shall live?" The groom gulped and looked around, and said in a tiny voice, "Yes." The groom leaned toward the minister and hissed, "I thought we had a deal." The minister put the $100 into his hand and whispered back, "She made me a much better offer."

16. Grandpa Jones was celebrating his 100th birthday and everybody complimented him on how athletic and well-preserved he appeared. "Gentlemen, I will tell you the secret of my success," he cackled. "I have been in the open-air day after day for some 75 years now." The celebrants were impressed and asked how he managed to keep up his rigorous fitness regime. "Well, you see my wife and I were married 75 years ago. On our wedding night, we made a solemn pledge. Whenever we had a fight, the one who was proved wrong would go outside and take a walk."

17. Once there was a millionaire, who collected live alligators. He kept them in the pool in the back of his mansion. The millionaire also had a beautiful daughter who was single. One day he decides to throw a huge party, and during the party he announces, "My dear guests . . . I have a proposition to every man here. I will give one million dollars or my daughter to the man who can swim across this pool full of alligators and emerge alive!" As soon as he finished his last word, there was the sound of a large splash!! There was one guy in the pool swimming with all he could and screaming out of fear. The crowd cheered him on as he kept stroking as though he was running for his life. Finally, he made it to the other side with only a torn shirt and some minor injuries. The millionaire was

impressed. He said, "My boy that was incredible! Fantastic! I did not think it could be done! Well I must keep my end of the bargain. Do you want my daughter or the one million dollars?" The guy says, "Listen, I don't want your money, nor do I want your daughter! I want the person who pushed me in that water!"

18. A minister was called to a local nursing home to perform a wedding. An anxious old man met him at the door. The pastor sat down to counsel the old man and asked several questions. "Do you love her?" The old man replied, "I guess." "Is she a good Christian woman?" "I don't know for sure," the old man answered. "Does she have lots of money?" asked the pastor. "I doubt it." "Then why are you marrying her?" the preacher asked. "She can drive at night," the old man said.

19. Your marriage is in trouble if your wife says, "You're only interested in one thing," and you cannot remember what it is.

20. Marriage is when a man and woman become as one. The trouble starts when they try to decide which one. Marriage is like a cage; one sees the birds outside desperate to get in, and those inside desperate to get out.

21. A young lady visited the government matchmaker for marriage and requested - "I'm looking for a spouse. Can you please help me to find a suitable one?" The marriage officer said, "Your requirements please." "Well, let me see. Needs to be good looking, polite, humorous, sporty, knowledgeable, good at singing and dancing. Willing to accompany me the whole day at home during my leisure hour if I don't go out. Telling me interesting stories when I need companion for conversation and be silent when I want to rest." The officer listened carefully and replied," I understand. You need a television."

22. A husband visited a marriage counselor and said, "When we were first married, I would come home from the office, my wife would bring my slippers and our cute little dog would run around barking. Now after ten years it is all-different. I come home, the dog brings the slippers and my wife runs around barking." "Why complain?" said the counselor, "You're still getting the same service."

23. "The thrill is gone from my marriage," Bill told his friend Doug. "Why not add some intrigue to your life and have an affair?" Doug suggested. "But what if my wife finds out?" "Heck, this is a new age we live in, Bill. Go ahead and tell her

about it!" So, Bill went home and said, "Dear, I think an affair will bring us closer together." "Forget it," said his wife. "I've tried that - it never worked."

24. Joe had asked Bob to help him out with the deck after work, so Bob just went straight over to Joe's place. When they got to the door, Joe went straight to his wife, gave her a hug, and told her how beautiful she was and how much he had missed her at work. When it was time for supper, he complimented his wife on her cooking, kissed her and told her how much he loved her. Once they were working on the deck, Bob told Joe that he was surprised that he fussed so much over his wife. Joe said that he had started this about 6 months ago, it had revived their marriage, and things couldn't be better. Bob thought he would give it a go. When he got home, he gave his wife a massive hug, kissed her and told her that he loved her. His wife burst into tears. Bob was confused and asked why she was crying. She said, "This is the worst day of my life. First, little Billy fell off his bike and twisted his ankle. Then, the washing machine broke and flooded the basement. And now, you come home drunk!"

25. A husband and wife were at a party chatting with some friends when the object of marriage counseling came up. "Oh, we'll never need that. My husband and I have a great

relationship," the wife explained. "He was a communications major in college, and I majored in theater arts. He communicates really well, and I just act like I'm listening."

We hope and trust that you have had some good time of laughter and healing. It is always great to have a cheerful heart and laugh with family and friends, especially your spouse. There is a time to laugh and there's a time not to. Be wise, willing, and watching.

Proverbs 15:13—*A joyful heart makes a cheerful face, but with a heartache comes depression.*

12

25 PRAYERS FOR MARRIAGES

Father in the name of Jesus grant grace to my spouse and help me be the encouragement to him. It is my prayer, it is my longing, that we may pass from this life together—a longing which shall never perish from the earth, but shall have place in the heart of every wife that loves, until the end of time; and it shall be called by my name. But if one of us must go first, it is my prayer that it shall be I; for he is strong, I am weak, I am not so necessary to him as he is to me—life without him would not be life; how could I endure it? This prayer is also immortal and will not cease from being offered up while my race continues. I am the first wife; and in the last wife I shall be repeated."—**Mark Twain, The Diaries of Adam and Eve**

Prayer is not just any work but the greater work. Prayer before, during and after marriage is essential to the success of every marriage home. Make it your goal and discipline to pray, pray and pray. Let us pray without ceasing and our marriage will keep seasoned.

Let our prayers cover the areas of protection, unity, forgiveness, conflict, God's presence, God's voice and but not limited to the following 25 areas.

1. Protection

"Be sober-minded; be watchful. Your adversary the devil prowls around like a roaring lion, seeking someone to devour. Resist him, firm in your faith, knowing that the same kinds of suffering are being experienced by your brotherhood throughout the world."—1 PETER 5:8-9

> Father, the enemy wants nothing more than to take our marriage down and stop the plans that You have for us. He knows that You want to use us for Your purposes in history and he wants to steal our joy. But we pray, in the name of Jesus, that You would protect us from the evil one and that You would cover our home and our relationship. In the good and the bad, in the ups and downs, we pray for security in You. We pray that You would even protect us from the harm that we could possibly do to ourselves knowingly or unknowingly. Help us to resist the enemy. Help us to stand strong in our faith. Make us steadfast in our pursuit of You and in pursuit of Your will. Be our shield, Lord Jesus, when

Satan attacks and be our refuge when we do not know where to turn. We place our full faith and confidence in You and Your love. We recognize that we will only find what we are looking for in You and we commit our lives to You.

2. Unity

"...with all humility and gentleness, with patience, bearing with one another in love, eager to maintain the unity of the Spirit in the bond of peace." —EPHESIANS 4:2-3

Dear God, we pray that we would be eager to maintain unity in our home. Teach us to bear with each in love in every circumstance we face. Thank You that in every decision and situation we have Your Word as our guide. In areas where the enemy would try to divide us, our finances, our careers, our time, our priorities, we pray that we seek Your will above our personal requests. Replace selfishness with humility, resentment with compassion, anger with gentleness, and conflict with peace. Make us one, Lord, in every area and in every decision. We submit our agenda for Your greater purpose. We let down our guard, surrender our desires and rely on Your strength to bind us together for Your eternal glory. Let our union exude Your presence and grow in us as a testimony of Your faithfulness.

3. Forgiveness

"For if you forgive others their trespasses, your heavenly Father will also forgive you, but if you do not forgive others their trespasses, neither will your Father forgive your trespasses."—MATTHEW 6:14-15

> Lord, though we fail You over and over again You are patient, gentle, and kind toward us. Thank You for Your faithful hand that leads us back to Your love and Your forgiveness and compassion that never runs out. May we live as a reflection of You, that may we deal with each other and those around us with compassion and gentleness. Teach us to forgive those around us like You have forgiven us. Help us to not allow resentment to build or unforgiveness to linger. Help us to extend grace and walk in humility as we acknowledge our need for Your constant flow of it in our lives. Help us to be a source of encouragement and replace condemnation with love and forgiveness.

4. Conflict

"The beginning of strife is like letting out water, so quit before the quarrel breaks out." —PROVERBS 17:14

Lord, You are holy. Thank You for the ever so gentle way that You deal with us. Give us the strength and self-control we need to show that same gentleness to each other. We know that You do not operate in chaos and confusion. Forgive us when we allow strife, bitterness, and worry to take root in our home and in our hearts. Teach us to control our temper and bring our attitudes under Your submission. Your Word tells us that there is power in our tongues, so we give You control over our unspoken and spoken words. God, we ask that You replace quarreling with compassion and resentment with joy. We are fully aware that arguments and dissension serve as distractions for the enemy to use to prevent us from resting in Your unending peace. At times when we desire to handle it ourselves, we ask that Your Holy Spirit would, remind us to leave our conflict at Your feet and seek You for resolve. Help us to bring every area of concern to You so that we can move forward in love.

5. *God's Presence*

"No one has ever seen God; if we love one another, God lives in us and his love is made complete in us." —1 JOHN 4:12

Dear Father, in the name of Jesus Christ, we thank You for the gift of marriage and for being the source of love. May our union be known by Your love. We pray that our actions toward each other would be an example of Your sacrifice and a result of Your presence. God, we give You permission to invade our home, take over our thoughts, and direct our paths. Be our strength when challenges come and remind us that it is the manifestation of Your Spirit that holds our union together. We ask that You give us the discipline we need to seek You daily and the boldness to live out Your plans. Abide in us. We rely on You and we are grateful for Your presence in our lives. We are fully dependent on Your presence and desire for our lives to be the evidence of Your love.

6. *Intimacy*

"Therefore, a man shall leave his father and his mother and hold fast to his wife, and they shall become one flesh."—GENESIS 2:24

Lord Jesus, we thank You that You have given us to each other in marriage and we pray that Your plan for us to be one flesh would be expressed in every area of life. Starting with our vows and commitments to each other, we pray for purity. We pray that we would honor each other completely and that we would put each other's needs in front of our own. Lord, grow a trust relationship between us that would be unbreakable. We pray that when others look at us, they would see You in us and a closeness in our union that doesn't come from the world. Reveal any false intimacy in our relationship and replace it with exactly what You had in mind when You created us for each other.

[Husband] Father, help me to love my wife like You love me and to give up even my life if You call me to do so. Until then, help me to die to any selfish way that would keep my wife from trusting and following me as I follow You.

[Wife] Lord, help me to respect my husband and trust that he has the good of our family in mind with every decision he makes. Help me to follow him as he follows You. Make us one as You are one.

7. Speak To Us

"He said, 'Blessed rather are those who hear the word of God and keep it!'" —LUKE 11:28

Father, in the name of Jesus Christ, we desire to hear Your voice and to follow Your ways. We pray that You would speak to us so that Your will, will be done through us. We seek You wholeheartedly, selflessly, and continually. Always help us to recognize Your voice and give us the courage we need to act on Your behalf. The busyness of life can get loud and there are distractions all around us. We know that it is the goal of the enemy to tempt us with the temporary pleasures of this world. Help us to stand together under You. Give us wisdom to know when to quiet the noise around us in order to hear You clearly. Grant us the patience to wait for You to speak when we are seeking Your voice. Help us to be confident as You guide our actions. Teach us to abide in Your presence, and most of all teach us to rest in the security of Your promises.

8. *Finances*

"Keep your life free from love of money, and be content with what you have, for he has said, 'I will never leave you nor forsake you.'"—HEBREWS 13:5

Lord, we seek to put You first in every area of our lives, including our finances. We are grateful for Your provision and the resources You have blessed us with. We ask that You use our finances as a source to bring us closer to You and not as a means of dissention or conflict. Help us to be of one mind with what we spend, how we save and how we give according to Your commands and desires. We do not cherish the treasures of this world, but we seek Your eternal blessings. Help us not to rely on Your resources but to trust You as our only Source. Your Word tells us that You will supply all our needs and we trust You for provision even when we do not see it. Help us to be content and faithful with our finances. We relinquish our control and selfish desires and come together under Your authority. Use everything that we have for Your kingdom.

9. Our Words

"Death and life are in the power of the tongue, and those who love it will eat its fruits."—PROVERBS 18:21

Lord, we are completely humbled when we think about the grandness of Your kingdom and the gifts You have chosen to give us. Of all the ways You could have given us to communicate, You chose to give man words. We are especially grateful for this gift. Unfortunately, we acknowledge that we do not always treat our words as a gift, and we are well aware of the damage our tongues can cause. Your Word tells us that our words are powerful and that our tongues have the ability to give life or to destroy it. Teach us to use our words to give life. Help us to keep quiet when we need to and to speak in love and gentleness when necessary. We desire that every part of our bodies be used as a vessel for Your glory and a testimony of Your goodness. Forgive us when we do not honor You with the things we say. We pray that You make our words gracious like a honeycomb that brings sweetness to the soul and health to the body. (Proverbs 16:24)

10. Friendships

"Iron sharpens iron, and one man sharpens another."— PROVERBS 27:17

Lord we thank You for our friendship. We are so grateful to have each other to enjoy and share life with. I pray that we never take our bond for granted. We ask that You protect our union. We also ask that You would, surround us with others who are seeking to build Your kingdom. We know that iron sharpens iron and we ask that You bring friends into our lives who will challenge us to grow, boldly speak truth into our lives, and seek Your wisdom on our behalf. Grant us the opportunities to serve others in this same way. We know that friendship is a gift and we ask that You help us to nurture, cherish, and protect those that You place in our paths.

11. *Spiritual Growth*

"From the day we heard, we have not ceased to pray for you, asking that you may be filled with the knowledge of his will in all spiritual wisdom and understanding, so as to walk in a manner worthy of the Lord, fully pleasing to him, bearing fruit in every good work and increasing in the knowledge of God." —COLOSSIANS 1:9-10

Heavenly Father, thank You that You have opened our eyes to see Your majesty and glory. We praise You for choosing us to be a part of Your kingdom family. We pray that You would continue to reveal Yourself to us in the fullness of Your grace and mercy. Help us to be likeminded in our pursuit of You, that we might, together, grasp the width, length, and height of Your love for us individually and within our marriage. We seek You for wisdom in our daily lives, turning to You in every decision, great or small. We ask that You would, help us to live in a way that is consistent with Your Word and the calling You have for our lives. May we please You in all that we do, always seeking what delights You, putting our desires to the side if they do not agree. And finally, as we grow in our affection and love for You, may all that we do bring about Your goodness and glory in the lives of others around us, that we would be conduits of Your truth and love to a culture around us that knows nothing of Your goodness.

12. Legacy

"Blessed is everyone who fears the LORD, who walks in his ways! You shall eat the fruit of the labor of your hands; you shall be blessed, and it shall be well with you. Your wife will be like a fruitful vine within your house; your children will be like olive shoots around your table. Behold, thus shall the man be blessed who fears the Lord. The Lord bless you from Zion! May you see the prosperity of Jerusalem all the days of your life! May you see your children's children! Peace be upon Israel!"— PSALM 128

Lord, thank You for the blessing and prosperity that are ours as we submit to You and as we walk like You would have us walk in our marriage. I pray that we would live every day in light of Your presence, knowing that keeping our eyes on You is the foundation of all that we are building together. May we always remember that our marriage is not just about us, but about what You are building and Your kingdom purposes. As we follow You, and as You pass down Your heavenly blessings to us, may we bless all those we touch. May all those in our household be fruitful, as an expression of Your Spirit living through us, that all who would come into contact with us benefit from our lives. Visit our home with Your blessings and prosperity that we might be conduits through which You bless others.

13. Thankful

"Give thanks in all circumstances; for this is the will of God in Christ Jesus for you."— 1 THESSALONIANS 5:18

Lord, we want to take time to say thank You. We are grateful for who You are and how Your presence has given us life. No matter what our circumstances look like from day today, we give You thanks. To say that we are nothing without You is an understatement. We are less than that. Yet, despite our nature, You choose to invade our lives and you seek to be one with us. You choose to bless us, and You choose to love us—thank You. Thank You for not allowing our sin to hold us hostage. Thank You for freedom from bondage and thank You that there is no shame. You start us afresh and grant us new mercies. Thank You that we do not have to work for Your love, but that You choose to love us freely. Thank You for Your protection, forgiveness, and unconditional love. Thank You for life. Help us to not take any good that we have for granted because we know that You are the only good in us.

14. Protection

"Be sober-minded; be watchful. Your adversary the devil prowls around like a roaring lion, seeking someone to devour. Resist him, firm in your faith, knowing that the same kinds of suffering are being experienced by your brotherhood throughout the world."—
1 PETER 5:8-9

Father, the enemy wants nothing more than to take our marriage down and stop the plans that You have for us. He knows that You want to use us for Your purposes in history and he wants to steal our joy. But we pray that You would protect us from the evil one and that You would cover our home and our relationship. In the good and the bad, in the ups and downs, we pray for security in You. We pray that You would even protect us from the harm that we could possibly do to ourselves knowingly or unknowingly. Help us to resist the enemy. Help us to stand strong in our faith. Make us steadfast in our pursuit of You and in pursuit of Your will. Be our shield, Lord Jesus, when Satan attacks and be our refuge when we do not know where to turn. We place our full faith and confidence in You and Your love. We recognize that we will only find what we are looking for in You and we commit our lives to You.

15. Obedience

"If you love me, you will keep my commandments."— JOHN 14:15

Lord, thank You for Your Word that clearly outlines what You expect from us—Your children. We love You and it is our heart's desire is to obey Your commands. We know that in our own power it is impossible to please You, so we ask that Your Holy Spirit will, give us the strength and discipline we need in order to live in full obedience of Your Word. Help us to live for You not simply with our hearts but through our actions. Teach us to obey immediately, fully, and without hesitation. We thank You for the gentle way that You guide us and lead us, and we pray that our lives will be a testimony of our love for You.

16. For Our Leadership

"For I have chosen him, that he may command his children and his household after him to keep the way of the LORD by doing

righteousness and justice, so that the Lord may bring to Abraham what he has promised him."— GENESIS 18:19

Jesus, thank You so much for bringing us together and for the promise that You will grow us and prosper us as we live in You. We commit our way to You and will make it our family's purpose to be a blessing to those we touch, starting with those in our home, and on to our neighbors and community. Lord, give us wisdom in our leadership. Teach us to be compassionate and gracious leaders of those that we have responsibility to shepherd. Give us diligence in our leadership. We are relying on You for the strength and the endurance to be consistent in how we exercise our authority. Most of all, continue to shape our hearts, that we might manage our home and areas of responsibility with love for those we are serving and overseeing. May we lead by example in Godly living, kindness, generosity, and fairness.

17. For Divine Direction

"Now the LORD said to Abram, 'Go from your country and your kindred and your father's house to the land that I will show you.'"— GENESIS 12:1

Father, thank You for the promise that we have in Your Word that You will lead and guide us and that You will continually take us to the destination that You have in mind for us. You have always led Your people and we pray, as Your people, that You would lead us toward that place. Lord, give us the mind of Christ that we might think like You think and that decisions will lead us toward Your will. Knowing that we will fail, we ask that Your grace will guide us even in our bad decisions. Order our steps and show us when to go one way or the other. And finally, use all our circumstances, the good, the bad, and the ugly, for our best and Your great purposes in history. Lord, we are waiting on You and trusting in Your plan through Your power for Your purpose today and forever.

18. For Our Health

"Beloved, I pray that all may go well with you and that you may be in good health, as it goes well with your soul."— 3 JOHN 1: 2

Lord, thank You that You care about our whole beings, body, mind, and spirit. We pray that we would live lives and have a marriage of balance, seeking to be spiritually healthy, first, which will lead to stronger mental and physical health. We pray that we would challenge each other to live healthy spiritual lives individually and that our relationship with You would drive each of us closer to You and into a more intimate walk with Jesus. We pray that we would sharpen each other mentally and that our activities and thought lives would lead to a stronger mental state to better discern and react to our environment around us. And lastly, we pray that we would honor our physical bodies, for each other and for our best service to You. Lord may Your grace make up the difference where we lack health and may You multiply our health for Your glory and our good.

19. Submission

"Submit yourselves therefore to God. Resist the devil, and he will flee from you." — JAMES 4:7

God, it is our heart's desire to submit our lives to You. We come seeking You for wisdom and asking for Your guidance. We know that it is impossible without Your help. Teach us what it looks like to personally die to ourselves daily in order to walk in full submission to You. We know that we cannot resist the traps and tricks of the enemy without You. So, we ask that You draw us into Your presence. We long to know You and to obey Your Word. Trusting that what You have for us is beyond anything we could ever imagine or earn; we surrender our will to Your way. We bring every area of our lives under Your authority and acknowledge You as Lord over our lives and all of creation.

20. *Unconditional Love*

"Love bears all things, believes all things, hopes all things, endures all things."— 1 CORINTHIANS 13:7

Father, thank You for giving us a true picture of what love looks like. Help us to take whatever preconceived or worldly definitions of love that we have and replace them with the truth of Your Word and true unconditional love in our marriage. We pray that our love would be patient with each other and slow to give up. Help us to be kind to each other, never lacking in compassion. We pray that our love would be good willed and always humble before each other. Help us to always speak highly of each other in private and in public. May Your grace in our lives cause us to be slow to take offense and quick to forgive with each opportunity. Lord, we pray that we would be each other's greatest shield, always defending each other from other people or situations that would attempt to cause us harm. And may we have an eternal optimism about our relationship and Your intent and purpose for bringing us together. Lord, bless our marriage. May it never fail, and may Your name be made great through it.

21. Our Time

"...making the best use of the time because the days are evil. Therefore, do not be foolish, but understand what the will of the Lord is." — EPHESIANS 5:16-17

> Lord, with each passing day we realize how precious and just how limited our time is. It is so easy for us to use it selfishly and foolishly, taking it for granted and treating it as if it were our own. We acknowledge that it is not. The time we have is a gift from You. Help us to steward it well and to give each moment we have back to You. Teach us to not base our actions on the limits of today and tomorrow but to live in light of eternity. We want to focus on the plans and purposes You have for Your people and specific roles and responsibilities You have planned for us to do. Reveal Your perfect will and help us to keep our focus on that which brings You glory.

22. Gifts

"As each has received a gift, use it to serve one another, as good stewards of God's varied grace."— 1 PETER 4:10

God, thank You for Your gifts and talents. You have blessed each of us with the talents needed to accomplish Your will, and more and more we realize just how uniquely designed we are as individuals. Your Word compares our lives as followers of You as individual parts of the same body. You created us for one purpose with a plan. The two of us are so distinctly different, yet when we come under Your authority those differences do not serve as hindrances but rather gifts to complement each other. Where one of us lacks, You have purposely given strength and direction to the other. God, we pray that You will teach us to function as one body. Help us to try to accomplish tasks that we were not created to do alone. Help us to the find joy in working together and give us the grace to follow You.

23. Our Perspective

"Be imitators of God, as beloved children. And walk in love, as Christ loved us and gave himself up for us, a fragrant offering and sacrifice to God."— EPHESIANS 5:1-2

Lord Jesus, thank You for Your life and what it means for our marriage. We pray that it may be a constant reminder of Your sacrifice, love, and duty and that we follow You fully in the pursuit of Christlike love. May we follow You in giving up our desires for the sake of each other. Help us to put aside personal wants and demands that get in the way of our oneness. Help us to die to these things, knowing that life will be produced in our marriage as a result. May we love selflessly, recklessly, and without reserve, looking at Your life as a model of perfect love for us. Though we are not perfect, we pray that Your grace would fill in the gaps and that our ability to express true love would grow increasingly. And may we be obedient to the calling You have placed on our marriage. You willingly went to the cross, giving all that You had for our benefit. Help us day by day and step by step to do the same in our pursuit of intimate relationship, that we might experience the delight and joy of knowing that we are both fully committed and that our love is here to stay.

24. A Place Of Refuge

"God is our refuge and strength, a very present help in trouble."—
PSALM 46:1-3

Lord, Your Word tells us that You are our refuge in times of trouble. God, trouble surrounds us, and it is our prayer that our home would become a place of refuge and safety in a lost and chaotic world. Satan is doing everything he can to prevent people from experiencing Your Love and the peace and joy that knowing You brings. Help us to open our doors selflessly and our hearts willingly to those who need to feel the security that comes from knowing You. Many of our friends, neighbors, and family are lost, burdened, and broken, and we ask that You use us and our home as a vessel to speak Your truth into their lives. Give us practical ways to serve and meet the needs of others, and may You shine through our actions. We seek You for strength and courage as we speak boldly to those You place before us and we thank You for the testimony of our union. May others find Your peace and rest in our home.

25. *Being Vulnerable With Each Other*

"There is no fear in love, but perfect love casts out fear. For fear has to do with punishment, and whoever fears has not been perfected in love."— 1 JOHN 4:18

Lord Jesus, You, are love and Your love is flawless. You are our example of how to love and look beyond fault. You knew our sin fully, but did not hold it against us, allowing us to live free from fear because Your love is perfect. Lord, though our love will never be perfect, we ask that You would grow us in our ability to love each other in a way that would create a safe environment for us to be known and to be free from fear of judgment or resentment from each other that the enemy would love to create. Bind us together in Your perfect love and give us a supernatural ability to live openly before each other and before You. Thank You, Lord, for the freedom You will give us in our marriage as we commit to knowing each other fully and loving just the same.

Hope you have enjoyed the prayers. We will request that you pray this bonus marriage prayer for strength and courage.

*Be strong and courageous. Do not be afraid or terrified because of them, for the L*ORD *your God goes with you; he will never leave you nor forsake you."*— DEUTERONOMY 31:6

Father, your greatest command was to love You and love each other. You've given marriage as a holy relationship that reflects our relationship with You. Show us how to follow your example and set aside our selfishness and pride and humbly serve each other. Help us to be of one spirit and of one mind and value each other above ourselves, looking out for each other's interests. In the midst of our busy lives, help us take time to love each other deeply from the heart, as you have loved us. May the love we have for each other be an example to the world of how You love them and gave Your life for them. Thank, you Father for granting us strength to love each other more and more, in Jesus name.

God loves you; we love you, so, let your love for God and for each other inspire you to pray without ceasing.

13

20 HONEST INSIGHTS ON MAKING IT TO 25 YEARS IN MARRIAGE

*We thought that this article by **Carey Nieuwhof** will add some honest insights to your marriage. Enjoy it.*

This month, my wife Toni and I celebrated 25 years of marriage. I love her more than I ever dreamed of. And it's also been a totally different experience than either of us thought it would be.

I love this picture of us leaving our wedding reception, because in many ways it shows us stepping out into the world when we honestly had NO IDEA what life would bring us. We just had hopes and dreams.

I have no data on this, but I think leaders perhaps struggle in their marriages more than others do.

Anecdotally, at least, I hear from leader after leader who says it's been tougher at home than they thought it would be. And Toni and I have had our share of struggles for sure.

If you're looking for a post on marriage that outlines how couples should do 5 things that will make their marriage perfect, you need to read someone else's blog.

The truth is marriage is work. Hard work. But it's wonderfully hard work. Both of us have felt more pain than we ever knew was possible, and more deep joy than we ever realized existed.

I love her more than I have ever loved anyone or anything (except Christ, of course). Our love has grown richer and better over time, but we've also had a few seasons where we wondered whether love had vaporized.

There were seasons where the only reason it was not over is because Jesus said it was not over. So, we stayed. And our emotions eventually caught up with our obedience. Through it all, Christ has kept us together and brought us a more wonderfully fulfilling relationship than either of us knew was possible.

On the other side of deep pain is deep joy. You have just got to make it there. So, what is the key?

Well, there is no one key, but here are 20 honest insights about making it to 25 years in marriage. Some are observations. Some are directives. Either way, I hope they help WHEREVER you are in your marriage.

1. Love Is A Decision, Not An Emotion

My dad always told me that love is an act of the will. He was right.

Culture says that love is an emotion. It is something you feel, not something you do. Culture could not be more wrong.

True love is a decision…a decision to place someone else's well being above yours. To stick through the tough times. To love when you do not feel love.

God is not thrilled with you all the time, yet he loves you. It is a decision, not an emotion.

♥ *Love is a decision, not an emotion.*

2. Your Emotions Eventually Catch Up To Your Obedience

There have been a few seasons in our 25 years where we stayed together simple because we were being obedient. (I would say Toni had to exercise her obedience more than I did.)

So, you stay when you feel like leaving. You stay when you feel like doing something irresponsible.

You just obey what you believe God has called you to do in the situation. I believe God has called me to stay married to one woman for life, and Toni believes God has called her to stay married to one man for life.

And in the process of being obedient, we both discovered something incredible: your emotions eventually catch up to your obedience.

Though the joy may have left for a few days, a few weeks, and once or twice, for a season, it came back. Deeper, richer and more abundant than we ever expected.

> ♥ *Your emotions eventually catch up to your obedience.*

3. Don't Make Tomorrow's Decisions Based On Today's Emotions

So you can see I've learned not to trust my feelings, because like the rest of creation, my feelings were victims of the fall.

A quick lesson: don't make tomorrow's decisions based on today's emotions.

Sometimes we defied stereotypical Christian advice and went to bed angry. But at least we went to bed together. And reason usually returned with the dawn.

Thank goodness on those days when emotion clouded judgment we just decided not to decide.

There's wisdom in that for life, not just for marriage.

> ♥ *Don't make tomorrow's decisions based on today's emotions. Decide not to decide.*

4. Live Your Story…Not Someone Else's

You will be tempted to compare yourself to other couples and other 'leadership' couples you admire. That can be healthy. It can also be horrible.

Live your story.

I've heard famous preachers say they've never had a fight about money. I promise you we have.

You can feel terrible about that and think "what's wrong with me?", or you can bring that before God and work it out together.

5. Instagram Lies

Nobody's life is as great as they make it out to be on Instagram.

If you're comparing your real life to someone else's posted life, you will implode.

Not much more to say about that. You know what I mean.

> ♥ *Nobody's life is a great as they make it out to be on Instagram.*

6. Don't Put Pressure On Your Spouse That Only God Can Bear

I heard this from Tim Keller a few years ago (do not have a source…sorry).

With the disappearance of God from more and more of our culture, people have lost a sense of the divine and the majestic.

Consequently, our desire to worship—no longer directed toward God—gets directed at our spouses and children. It places pressure on them they were not designed to bear, and many marriages and families collapse from the pressure.

Pinterest has placed a ridiculous amount of pressure on wedding receptions and even home decor that the average family can't live up to. The kind of majesty that used to go into a cathedral now goes into a two-year old's birthday party.

There is something fundamentally flawed with this, and the sooner you take that pressure off your spouse, off your kids and off yourself, the healthier you become.

> ♥ *Do not put pressure on your spouse that only God can bear.*

7. You Probably Married Your Opposite

All those things you loved about your spouse when you were dating are the some of the things that will drive you crazy when you are married.

We just get attracted to our opposites.

Knowing that is progress in itself and will help you delight in your spouse (when he or she isn't driving you crazy over said opposites).

8. Counsellors Are Worth It

Toni and I first started seeing a counsellor when we were in our mid-thirties. I should have gone when I was in my twenties.

I do not know where I'd be as a person, husband, father and leader without the help I've had from some incredible Christian counsellors who have helped me see where I need grace and redemption.

I resisted going to counselling. If you are resisting, stop. There's freedom on the other side.

9. Progress Starts When You See That You're The Problem

We had a great couple of first years, but when tension arose, I thought none of it was my fault.

After all, I had little conflict as a single guy, so who had to be bringing all this tension in my marriage? Could not have been me.

I could not have been more wrong.

Now I just assume I am probably the problem. And I usually am. It is simpler that way…in life and leadership.

10. Your Unspoken Assumptions Can Sink You

There is a right way and a wrong way to do everything…or so we think.

In the kitchen, I take an ingredient out, and then I put it back. And wipe the counter. Then I take the next step in cooking whatever I am cooking.

Toni takes everything out, makes a glorious meal, and cleans up later when the food is cooking.

I assumed my way was the right way. But there is no right and wrong here, just different.

Yet we did not know what was driving our kitchen tension until we named it. Now we can laugh at it (most days).

When you surface the assumptions…you mitigate the conflict.

11. When You Agree On Values, You'll Agree A Lot More

Because it is often the little things you fight about, it's important to understand where you agree on the big things.

Big things would include your faith, your approach to parenting, your philosophy of life, your priorities, your finances and more.

When you agree on your values, you will agree on a lot more.

12. Remember That If You Leave, You Take All Your Unresolved Problems To Your Next Relationship

This is simply true, and you have seen it 1000 times in others.

And you think you will be the exception to the rule.

You will not be.

13. Pray Together

Pray together. Out loud.

Yes, it is hard. Yes, it is awkward.

Yes, men resist it. And yes, pastors resist it.

Do it.

14. If You are A Guy, Lead Your Marriage Spiritually

My wife and I met in law school. A progressive, left-leaning law school.

Had I even suggested in any way that I was the spiritual head of a home, I would have been laughed out of the school. Or maybe arrested.

But 25 years in, there is no question I need to lead my wife spiritually. My leadership needs to reflect Christ's leadership (a servant's attitude motivated by love), but it is still leadership.

Most men resist taking spiritual leadership at home. Most male leaders resist taking authentic, Christ-motivated loving leadership at home.

Start leading in love.

15. Go On Weekly Date Nights

In the early days we had no money for date nights. We went anyway.

When your kids are young, it is especially important because most of your conversation is 'transactional' (you cook…I will drive the kids to soccer).

In the rough seasons, sometimes we would spend the first half of date night resolving arguments we could not finish in the hum of everyday life. Not fun, but probably healthy.

But we had some awesome date nights too.

Do not have time? Do not have money?

Well, if you broke up, you would date your new girlfriend.

So instead, date your wife. Your kids will thank you for it.

You will thank yourself for it one day too.

> ♥ *If you broke up, you would date your new girlfriend. So, husbands, date your wife.*

16. Don't Make Your Kids The Centre Of Your Family

In today's culture, kids have become the centre of many homes.

Parents have stopped living for Christ and for each other and started basing all their decisions around their kids.

There are two problems with that.

First, your kids eventually leave…leaving you with a gaping hole.

Second, putting your kids at the centre of your home communicates to them that they are more important than they are. And they know it. As Tim Elmore has suggested, this approach produces kids with high arrogance and low self-esteem.

Child-centered parenting produces self-centred kids.

The best gift you can give your kids is a Christ-centered, healthy marriage.

> ♥ *Child-centered parenting produces self-centered children.*

17. Take Personal Vacations Without The Kids

We were one of the few couples among our friends who did this, but every year Toni and I would get away even for a night or two WITHOUT the kids.

Our friends would tell us it had been 3, 5 even 10 years since they had done it.

I am so glad we took the time to do that. It renewed and remade us. We made significant progress on our relationships so many times we did that. Plus…so much of it was fun.

18. Take Family Vacations Every Year

We also took family vacations every year. Often, they were not glorious. We did what we could afford.

But our kids (now 23 and 19) tell us it was one of their favourite things growing up and something that really bonded our family.

I wrote more about why and how we took those vacations in this Parent Cue post.[8]

Bottom line? You do not have to go to Disney…you just have to go.

---

[8] http://theparentcue.org/why-family-vacations-need-to-be-a-non-negotiable/

19. Figure Out How To Be A Couple Again Before Your Kids Grow Up

When our then 16-year-old drove off in the car with his brother on the day he got his driver's licence, Toni and I were left standing in the living room waving good-bye.

Then we looked at each other and said, "Oh my goodness…before we know it, they're going to be gone."

We realized we had WAY more life ahead of us where it would just be us.

So, we started new hobbies we could enjoy together (snowshoeing, hiking, cycling) and really worked on our friendship.

My favourite thing to do on my days off is to hang out with my best friend.

20. Open The Gift Of Sex…It's From God

There's so much funk about sex. For the record, I believe marriage is the context God designed for sex.

The irony of course is that too many married couples lose interest in sex. I have met way too many people who tell me (because I'm a pastor I guess) that they live in a sexless marriage.

Significantly, our culture only glamorizes sex outside of marriage.

When was the last time you saw a married couple on TV or in a movie in a love scene? Right…you cannot remember.

You are probably even thinking gross, I would not want to see that. (Not that any of us should be watching steamy scenes, but you get the point).

And now you see the problem.

Why, in our culture, is it not weird when a couple at a bar in a movie hooks up or a wife whose husband is out of town gets it on with her boss, but it is weird when two people who have committed to each other for life have sex?

Why?

Married people: sex is a gift. Open it.

The more emotionally, relationally, and spiritually close you get to your spouse, the better it gets.

14

CONCLUSION

In conclusion read through proverbs 31, pay attention to the virtue and reject the vice.

31 The sayings of King Lemuel—an inspired utterance his mother taught him.

² Listen, my son! Listen, son of my womb!
   Listen, my son, the answer to my prayers!
³ Do not spend your strength on women,
   your vigor on those who ruin kings.

⁴ It is not for kings, Lemuel—
   it is not for kings to drink wine,
   not for rulers to crave beer,
⁵ lest they drink and forget what has been decreed,
   and deprive all the oppressed of their rights.
⁶ Let beer be for those who are perishing,
   wine for those who are in anguish!

⁷ Let them drink and forget their poverty
  and remember their misery no more.

⁸ Speak up for those who cannot speak for themselves,
  for the rights of all who are destitute.
⁹ Speak up and judge fairly;
  defend the rights of the poor and needy.

Epilogue: The Wife of Noble Character

¹⁰ A wife of noble character who can find?
  She is worth far more than rubies.
¹¹ Her husband has full confidence in her
  and lacks nothing of value.
¹² She brings him good, not harm,
  all the days of her life.
¹³ She selects wool and flax
  and works with eager hands.
¹⁴ She is like the merchant ships,
  bringing her food from afar.
¹⁵ She gets up while it is still night;
  she provides food for her family
  and portions for her female servants.
¹⁶ She considers a field and buys it;
  out of her earnings she plants a vineyard.

[17] She sets about her work vigorously;
> her arms are strong for her tasks.

[18] She sees that her trading is profitable,
> and her lamp does not go out at night.

[19] In her hand she holds the distaff
> and grasps the spindle with her fingers.

[20] She opens her arms to the poor
> and extends her hands to the needy.

[21] When it snows, she has no fear for her household;
> for all of them are clothed in scarlet.

[22] She makes coverings for her bed;
> she is clothed in fine linen and purple.

[23] Her husband is respected at the city gate,
> where he takes his seat among the elders of the land.

[24] She makes linen garments and sells them,
> and supplies the merchants with sashes.

[25] She is clothed with strength and dignity;
> she can laugh at the days to come.

[26] She speaks with wisdom,
> and faithful instruction is on her tongue.

[27] She watches over the affairs of her household
> and does not eat the bread of idleness.

[28] Her children arise and call her blessed;
> her husband also, and he praises her:

²⁹ "Many women do noble things,

   but you surpass them all."

³⁰ Charm is deceptive, and beauty is fleeting;

   but a woman who fears the LORD is to be praised.

³¹ Honor her for all that her hands have done,

   and let her works bring her praise at the city gate.

Oh man, stay away from women, drunkenness, and injustice. Woman be virtuous, selfless, submissive and sacrificial. Oh, husband and wife; love, submit, support, and respect each other.

♥♥♥♥♥♥♥♥♥♥♥

The five-finger illustration from the factors that make a great entrepreneur in the "*Midas Touch*", I believe can appropriately apply to healthy lasting long marriages. Your marriage Will thrive, be healthy, strong, and lasting when it is built on these factors or critical attributes: The thumb represents strength of character-this enables you stand the test of time, index finger- focus-this keeps you as a team and one, middle finger-the brand- what you stand for, ring finger-relationships- this you must continue to develop and deepen, and last but not the least, little finger is about the little things that if ignored can become the big things that might end the marriage.

The determined marriage couple's ability to dream, win, lose, win, dream and win again and again is called the marriage spirit. Great marriage couples see the future together, dream it, risk it, try out, fail, lose, win, fail and win. Arise as two lovers, and fight, fail, lose, win, fail and win and win again.

We declare that:

[25] *Now all glory to God, who is able to make you strong, just as my Good News says. This message about Jesus Christ has revealed his plan for you Gentiles, a plan kept secret from the beginning of time.* [26] *But now as the prophets foretold and as the eternal God has commanded, this message is made known to all Gentiles everywhere, so that they too might believe and obey him.* [27] *All glory to the only wise God, through Jesus Christ, forever. Amen.* — Romans 16:25-27

APPENDIX 1

List of marriages reported to be more than 80 years

Hope this list encourages you to keep your marriage for life:

Names	Marriage date	Length of marriage	End date (person's death)	Residence (at date of last report or death)	Notes
Karam Chand Kartari Chand	11 December 1925	90 years, 291 days	30 September 2016 (Karam)	Bradford (England), United Kingdom	Not recognized by Guinness World Records[15]
K. Philipose Thomas Sosamma Thomas	17 February 1918	88 years, 2 days	19 February 2006 (Sosamma)	Kerala, India	Not recognized by Guinness World Records[13]
Herbert Fisher, Sr. Zelmyra (née George) Fisher	13 May 1924	86 years, 290 days	27 February 2011 (Herbert)	North Carolina, United States	Current Guinness World Record for longest marriage, recognized in 2008[10][21]

Names	Marriage date	Length of marriage	End date (person's death)	Residence (at date of last report or death)	Notes
Temulji Bhicaji Nariman Lady Nariman	1853	86 years	1 August 1940 (Temulji)	Maharashtra, India	Temulji and Lady Nariman married as cousins when they were 5 years old. This was noted as longest marriage recorded through 1940. Shared Guinness World Record with Lazarus and Mary Rowe for editions up to 1998.[9]
Lazarus Rowe Mary (née Webber) Rowe	1743	86 years	27 June 1829 (Mary)	New Hampshire, United States	Shared Guinness World Record with the Narimans for editions up to 1998[9]
Liu Yung-Yang Liu Yang Yang-Wan	1917	86 years	21 July 2003 (Yang Yang-Wan)	Taoyuan, Taiwan	Was recognized by *Guinness World Records 2004* (published in 2003) as world's longest marriage[30][31]
John George Betar Ann (née Shawah) Betar	25 November 1932	85 years, 291 days	12 September 2018 (John)	Connecticut, United States	Winner of the Worldwide Marriage Encounter's Longest Married Couple Project in 2013[12]
Duranord Veillard Jeanne Hermina Veillard	29 November 1932	85 years, 184 days	1 June 2018 (Duranord)	New York, United States	

Names	Marriage date	Length of marriage	End date (person's death)	Residence (at date of last report or death)	Notes
Maurice Kaye Helen Kaye	27 August 1934	83 years, 330 days	22 July 2018 (Maurice)	Bournemouth (England), United Kingdom	
Henry Andrew Johnson Lena (née Knudsen) Johnson	8 February 1920	83 years, 231 days	27 September 2003 (Lena)	Iowa, United States	
William B. Ritchie Claudia Lillian Ritchie	12 April 1919	83 years, 224 days	22 November 2002 (William)	Kentucky, United States	Recognized by Guinness World Records as world's oldest living married couple in 2002
Norman James Burmah Norma "Mickey" (née Depland) Burmah	27 January 1931	83 years, 222 days	6 September 2014 (Norma)	Louisiana, United States	
Marshall N. Kuykendall Winifred Louisiana "Winnie Louise" (née Macnab) Kuykendall	14 February 1929	83 years, 221 days	22 September 2012 (Winnie)	New Mexico, United States	Winner of the Worldwide Marriage Encounter's inaugural Longest Married Couple Project in 2011[12]
Steven "Steve" Wrubel Victoria Virginia "Vicky" (née Puvalowski) Wrubel	28 September 1929	83 years, 192 days	8 April 2013 (Vickie)	Florida, United States	Were recognized by Guinness World Records in 2011, but did not clinch the record[42]

Names	Marriage date	Length of marriage	End date (person's death)	Residence (at date of last report or death)	Notes
George L. Briant Germaine (née Thibodeaux) Briant	20 July 1921	83 years, 192 days	25 January 2005 (Germaine) 28 January 2005 (George)	Louisiana, United States	Honored by Governor David Vitter in the Louisiana Family Forum's inaugural Louisiana's longest married couple contest in 2004
Masao Matsumoto Miyako Sonoda	20 October 1937	81 years, 209 days	17 May 2019 (Masao)	Kagawa, Japan	Guinness World Record for "Oldest living married couple, aggregate age", recognized in August 2018[45] Guinness World Record for "Oldest married couple, aggregate age" (17 May 2019)[a]
Michael Nikolaus Katharina Nikolaus	26 December 1924	80 years, 358 days	19 December 2005 (Katharina)	Siegen, Germany	
Loyd Monroe Collins Evelyn Eunice (née Garlington) Collins	11 August 1934	80 years, 334 days	10 July 2015 (Evelyn)	Louisiana, United States	Recognized by the Louisiana Family Forum in 2012
Ronald Gilbert Collings Esther Elizabeth Collings	19 October 1938	80 years, 187 days	24 April 2019 (Esther)	Adelaide, Australia	Australia's oldest couple mark 80 years together[56]

Names	Marriage date	Length of marriage	End date (person's death)	Residence (at date of last report or death)	Notes
Arend Noordhuis Aaltje (née Nijstad) Noordhuis	22 January 1938	82 years, 193 days		Drenthe, Netherlands	
John Henderson Charlotte (née Curtis) Henderson	22 December 1939	80 years, 224 days		Texas, United States	Recognized by Guinness Word Records as the oldest living married couple.
Warren Clinton Snell Arlene Larson	25 February 1940	80 years, 159 days		Iowa, United States	
Lukas De Jong Eva Bakker	27 May 1940	80 years, 67 days		California, United States	
Jon Magnusson Rita Magnusson	14 July 1940	80 years, 19 days		Hvidovre, Denmark	

BIBLIOGRAPHY

1. https://www.timesofisrael.com/jewish-liberator-of-nazi-camp-wife-of-78-years-die-hours-apart/?
2. Excerpt from: *"Marriage and Divorce: The New Testament Teaching"* by B. Ward Powers. Scribd Edition.
   https://www.scribd.com/book/335710015
3. *Sue Schlesman is a Christian writer, teacher, and speaker. Her blogs, fiction, and non-fiction reach a wide audience. You can find her philosophizing about life, education, family, and Jesus at www.susanwalleyschlesman.com and www.7prayersthatwork.com.*
4. **Source (30 Days of marriage prayers by Tony Evans)**
5. https://www.crosswalk.com/family/marriage/20-reasons-marriages-fail-even-christian-marriages.html
6. https://www.marriage.com/advice/divorce/10-most-common-reasons-for-divorce/
7. https://www.essence.com/love/relationships/most-overlooked-reasons-marriages-fail/
8. https://www.beliefnet.com/love-family/relationships/marriage/6-reasons-christian-marriages-fail.aspx
9. https://www.wiseoldsayings.com/life-lessons-quotes/#ixzz6RdWI1Zpr
10. https://www.biblword.net/a-christian-marriage/?gclid
11. https://www.cnn.com/2019/10/19/opinions/jimmy-carter-rosalynn-carter-long-marriage-drexler/index.html
12. https://www.huffpost.com/entry/the-top-7-reasons-why-marriages-last_b_5a0af523e4b00652392183db

13. http://jokes.christiansunite.com/Marriage/Why_Men_Can't_Win.shtml
14. http://www.sarasotawedding.com/jokes/marriage_jokes.html
15. https://www.bing.com/search?q=marriage+quotes+love&q
16. https://abcnews.go.com/Lifestyle/couples-married-longer-50-years-spill-secret-long/story?id=45222748
17. https://bestlifeonline.com/long-marriage-secrets/
18. John B. Ghartey. Marriage Means More, Living Word Foundations, Accra, Ghana. 2009.

Love is beyond sex and physical touch. Love is kind words, a reassuring smile, one that is not jealous, and keeps record of wrong doings. Love is knowing without a shadow of a doubt that you will always be there for that person and they will always be there for you.

—*Marriage.com*

SECRETS OF HAPPY COUPLES

1. THEY RECOGNIZE AND RESPOND TO EACH OTHER'S BIDS FOR ATTENTION
2. THEY PRIORITIZE INTIMACY AND SEX
3. THEY SHOW INTEREST IN EACH OTHER'S WORLDS BY ASKING QUESTIONS
4. THEY SUPPORT EACH OTHER'S GROWTH AND LEARNING OF NEW THINGS
5. THEY SEE PROBLEMS AS JOINT PROBLEMS TO BE SOLVED

The Gottman Institute

OUR FAMILY

We will **love and accept** one another.
> *Romans 14:1, Romans 15:7, 1 Peter 1:22, I John 4:7*

We will **pray** for one another.
> *Philippians 1:3-4, 1 Timothy 2:1, Hebrews 13:7, James 5:16*

We will **tell the truth** to each other.
> *Ephesians 4:25, Colossians 3:9, 1 Peter 2:1, 1 Peter 3:10*

We will **be kind** to one another.
> *Zechariah 7:9, Colossians 3:12, 1 Thessalonians 5:15*

We will **bring joy** to each other
> *Proverbs 15:30, Proverbs 17:22, Proverbs 23:25, Philemon 1:7*

We will **serve** one another.
> *Acts 20:35, James 1:27, 1 Peter 4:10, 1 Peter 5:5*

We will **be patient** with each other
> *1 Cor. 12:12-25, Ephesians 4:2, Colossians 3:13, James 1:19-20*

We will **comfort** one another
> *2 Corinthians 1:3-7, Galatians 6:2, 2 Thessalonians 2:16-17*

We will **forgive** one another
> *Luke 6:36-37, Luke 17:3-4, Colossians 3:13, I Peter 3:9*

We will **be generous** with each other

> *Proverbs 22:9, Acts 2:42-47, 1 Timothy 6:17-19, 1 Peter 4:9*

We will **honor** each other

> *Mark 9:35, Romans 12:10, Philippians 2:3, 1 Peter 2:17*

www.ingramcontent.com/pod-product-compliance
Lightning Source LLC
Chambersburg PA
CBHW060825050426
42453CB00008B/592